CAPRICORN

1999

TOTAL HOROSCOPE

♑ DEC 21 – JAN 19 ♑

J

JOVE BOOKS, NEW YORK

The publishers regret that they cannot answer individual
letters requesting personal horoscope information.

1999 TOTAL HOROSCOPE: CAPRICORN

PRINTING HISTORY
Jove edition / July 1998

The Penguin Putnam Inc. World Wide Web site address is
http://www.penguinputnam.com

ISBN: 0-515-12313-7

A JOVE BOOK®
Jove Books are published by The Berkley Publishing Group,
a member of Penguin Putnam Inc.,
200 Madison Avenue, New York, New York 10016.
JOVE and the "J" design
are trademarks belonging to Jove Publications, Inc.

PRINTED IN THE UNITED STATES OF AMERICA

10 9 8 7 6 5 4 3 2 1

CONTENTS

MESSAGE TO CAPRICORN

Dear Capricorn,

Capricorn is depth. You gain strength not from rushing from one job to the next, but from staying with a problem until it is solved. When you are jumpy, anxious, and unsettled, you need structure in your life, something to focus on and to which you can devote your efforts. Although you are secretly a dreamer, the major aim in your life is to deepen yourself in a given area, whatever you have chosen. If you are career-oriented, you move forward slowly, gaining experience, power, and position, always digging deeper into your work, learning, experiencing, climbing carefully, slipping here and there but never falling. You may lose ground, encounter setbacks, but each obstacle makes you more aware of the steps ahead.

You rarely feel you have already made it. You don't boast that you've arrived, because you are aware of how much farther you have to go. It is the slow, sure climb to the top that you are involved in, not simply the flash and pomp of enjoying the crown.

Capricorns may have experienced sudden reversals and changes in career status, professional upheavals, scandals, and anxieties, and unexpected events through their partners or other people. Many Capricorns have changed goals suddenly, left jobs, and no longer feel career or success-oriented at all. Actually, Capricorns try to remain relatively unchanged by upheavals. You like to feel impervious to bombardment from strange or alien forces. You are reluctant to have existing rules and patterns broken—rules and patterns that give your life endurance, safety, and stability. But when the up-heaval and shouting is over, Capricorn may return to a safer, narrower point of view and enjoy the fruits of expanded experience and new visions of life. The development of the personal self will be achieved through that word mentioned earlier: depth.

If you are a homemaker, you're probably the greatest shopper to stalk the supermarket. If you're a movie star, you're ageless and irreplaceable. If you're a philosopher or scientist, you go to the heart of every question that arises. If you're into money, your mind is a busy cash register. You're an eager executive, smooth politician, ruthless dictator. You always affect the Establishment in some way. You are corruptible in your love of control. Otherwise you are generous, philosophical, talented, and wise. Whatever you do, if you're a Capricorn and happy, you do it well.

You'll often run into Capricorns who really don't achieve much or feel satisfaction or pride in the things they do. They are sloppy, irrational, and over-emotional. Yes, overemotional! Capricorns often disapprove so strongly of being deep and sensible, they will live their lives being unreasonable, irresponsible, and careless. They are actually trying to find a balance between what they have been told all their lives they should be, and what they feel they should become. So they go on a reckless binge and later turn into sober, serious, sometimes cynical people. You may know people who do this who aren't Capricorns. But a deeper analysis of their horoscopes will show the influence of Capricorn in their lives.

You may feel that you have to be too serious and too responsible. Nobody likes to feel like a robot or a machine. Often you must throw off the burdens and sober frame of reference of your daily life and have a wild fling, an adventure just for the fun of it, to let yourself know there's a world out there with interesting things to see and learn. You won't be happy until you find a balance between your emotional self and your mental self. Often you'll attract people because of your stability and responsibility. You think at first they're going to mother you and take care of you. After a while you find yourself guarding and taking care of them. If they become too loving or motherly, you may reject them as weak or lazy. You can't resist the fruitful, artistic side of people, while at the same time you criticize an artistic way of life as unrespectable or unpredictable. This is one of your conflicts.

You crave security and emotional sustenance in a relationship, yet you often find it difficult to accept unlimited love, affection, and feeling from another human being. While you are soothed and bathed by the warmth another can bring you, many times you feel inhibited or prohibited from accepting it, for one practical reason or another. Whatever the reason, you believe that structure is necessary to life. You must define your emotional life in terms of limits, in the way the size and shape of a swimming pool will determine the exact amount of water it will hold.

If you know yourself well and recognize your needs, if you meet your emotions honestly and don't fear being inundated by them, you can find a loving, affectionate partner for a long-lasting, happy, successful relationship. If you are reluctant to look deep within yourself, the results can be disastrous. You are fiercely loyal and will blind your eyes to many of your partner's shortcomings when it comes to defending him or her against the outside world. You can be like a fort full of soldiers protecting the women and children inside from attack. Internally, though, things could be terribly different. You often hold things in and don't let anything inside get out and be free. When you are emotionally frightened, you close up. The reaction is chaos, coldness, separation, and the demise of what could be a beautiful marriage. It's a dilemma. If you could give yourself up totally to your emotions, without any thought of being reasonable, you'd end up having to work harder than before. Then you would have practical reasons to turn off romance.

In no way does this mean you lack the capacity to love someone. It simply signifies another aspect to love between two people. Love for the Capricorn is faith, devotion, loyalty, steadfastness, duty, reality, and deep underlying responsibility. If you pretend not to have a brain, the results will be so chaotic that you will eventually find it necessary to retreat into coldness, diffidence, and icy distance.

You can be an iceberg, to be sure. You are calculating, shrewd, stiff, unforgiving. You are manipulative and pragmatic and will use others when necessary. You often lack true sympathy, especially when you feel you are being invaded. There's a social climber in you with a stingy, disagreeable bitterness that can make you a dry, uncompromising rightwinger. You can use your tremendous capacity for organization and skillful diplomacy with people as a tool for the acquisition of power. You can sometimes enjoy controlling people and situations to the exclusion of genuine human feeling. When it suits you, you can turn off emotions and find undeniable reasons for doing so.

But the quality about you as a Capricorn that everyone needs in order to make a success out of anything— love or career—is the depth of understanding and patience that makes you what you are. If you will only give yourself over to developing it, you will be a master of understanding. What you lack in luster and fire, you make up for in profundity.

During the part of the year when the Sun is in the sign of Capricorn, Earth comes closest to the Sun. But the North Pole tips away from the Sun, so that we in the northern part of the globe are tipped away from the light. Thus nights are longer. Life slows down. The sap stays in the trees, the animals are hushed in their nests and caves with all the necessary food stored up for long nights ahead. Winter begins here, and there is a patient wait for the Earth to begin to tip toward the Sun again. There is no depression or hopelessness in the trees or animals. Something deep within them knows that spring will come this year as it does every year.

Capricorns do have the patience and endurance to wait for what they want. Their successes are often long in coming, but they do come, sure as springtime. But you often meet Capricorns who are hopeless and depressed, dark and gloomy, who dwell on trouble and sorrow. They seem to have replaced patience with despair. They have thrown out determination and live in narrow-minded poverty of the spirit.

You are Capricorn because you enjoy a certain comfort in aligning your aims and ambitions with the restrictions that prevent success, and then achieving success despite those restrictions. You lose valuable time when you dwell on the obstacle instead of the power within you to grow and succeed under the shadow of that obstacle. Your least attractive qualities are your downhearted tendency, which can discourage and deter people from their dreams, and your cynical yet controlling tendency to stand in someone's way. Your contribution is the helpful and loving understanding you can provide in pointing out certain inescapable facts, and then the way you go about removing any obstacles that might impede progress.

It is quite true that your life has responsibilities and burdens that others' may not have. But you choose a way of living that is most comfortable for you. You will ultimately feel best in accepting the role of responsible authoritarian, because in that way you can exercise your unbeatable qualities for problem solving.

If you are too conscious of your limitations and lack the confidence to carry out your goals, what is the source of your discouragement? Often you may have had a difficult childhood and may have lived with conditions and situations that impeded you from realizing your goals. There may have been poverty, or sickness, or problems in the environment that could not be erased, always bringing you down and keeping you from doing what you wanted to do. You may have had a parent who was critical or disapproving or even absent and not there to support you in your endeavors. There could be a problem of social condition, reputation, or prestige that caused you pain, embarrassment, or depression. Whatever the reason, you as a Capricorn must use that very limitation as the building block to your success as a mature adult.

You're often old when you're young, and then you grow into your skin as time goes on. As a child, if you weren't weak or sickly, there was probably a quality of the older person in you. The influence of elderly people and Father Time seems to be connected quite directly with Capricorn. Your skin may wrinkle early, or your hair may turn gray. But as time goes on, your well-conserved youth will begin to blossom long after the Sun has set for many of your contemporaries. If you worry too much about what may happen in the future, you miss all the fun of the present. If you are too worried about getting old, you never experience the heady carelessness of being young. What seems to be over-seriousness and overconcern with practicality in your youth will be the fruits of maturity in later years.

In one sense you're a born professional, with a capacity for self-discipline that will keep you in shape all the way to the top. Your teeth, bones, skin, knees, and joints are your major health areas with their reflex results on head, stomach, kidneys, and lower back. Good diet, hard work, and exercise are your tools to remaining healthy. Your occasional binges are necessary since so much of the time you try not to allow yourself indulgences and naughty luxuries. People wouldn't believe it from talking to you, but you are really quite indulgent, with a stronger taste for all kinds of pleasures than you allow yourself to admit.

You're surprisingly charitable about money. You often feel disappointment or confusion when dealing with brothers and sisters. You are ever striving to free yourself from parental or childhood programing. You're a great pleasure lover and you enjoy lavish good times, although you can't stop worrying about the expense, even if it isn't yours. In work you are bright, quick-minded, and easy to get along with on a superficial level. Although you are often restless, flighty, and easily bored, you conquer this boredom through persistence, determination, and concentration. When you devote yourself to a problem you are profound, thorough, imaginative, talented, and original. You can attack it from all angles at once so that the problem doesn't have a chance against your searching deliberate action. You're economical and thrifty, sometimes too stingy and callous, but with a natural dislike of waste and a mistrust of exaggeration.

The future frightens you because you fear the adoption of beliefs or codes of ethics that will undermine either your importance or your sense of values—both of which have been structured according to social conformity. Your strength and staying power are almost unmatchable. While many others would have surrendered long ago, you're just getting started. The hotter it gets around you, the cooler you become.

Sexually you can be a lot warmer than anyone would imagine. You could be bold, dashing, and astonishingly ardent. You can be an exotic, glamorous lover, sometimes too much concerned with the image you are making, but able to handle your powerful passions and desires. Like everything else, when you decide to do it, you've got to be the best.

You're always striving to perfect and purify your understanding of yourself and the world in general. Your code of conduct, although strictly pragmatic, is aiming at honesty, helpfulness, and sincere self-improvement. Your highest aims, strangely enough, often are not involved with career or profession. Your highest success often comes in the area of marriage. It gives you the feeling of greatest accomplishment.

You don't often show it immediately, but you are vastly more sensitive than you dare let on, and this can turn you inward. Then you set up outside defenses while you examine and reexamine your inside self.

In a way, you are like a well-constructed pyramid: perfect and architecturally correct, mysteriously implacable, very hard to know. You are organized to a high degree, have been built to last and last and last. You are practical and useful, yet magnificently dignified, signifying permanence and finality and reflecting careful planning from the beginning.

Like the pyramid, laid stone by stone, you are successful only after great effort. When you get to the top, you can be pretty narrow. Yet you are the eternal riddle of beauty, the paradox of the ages, complete with properties no one will ever know.

Michael Lutin

CAPRICORN SNEAK PREVIEW
OF THE 21st CENTURY

As the last decade of the twentieth century comes to a close, planetary aspects for its final years connect you with the future. Major changes completed in 1995 and 1996 form the bridge to the twenty-first century and new horizons. The years 1997 through 1999 and into the year 2000 reveal hidden paths and personal hints for achieving your potential, your message from the planets.

Capricorn individuals, ruled by wise planet Saturn, are experiencing great activity and profound change. A major shift in your life is coming from Pluto in Sagittarius, already under way since November 1995. Pluto in Sagittarius till the year 2007 urges you to confront basic truths. The past must be put into perspective so you can reach your potential. Your ruling planet Saturn goes through two cycles in the late '90s significant to your journey into the future.

Saturn in fiery Aries April 1996 to March 1999 marks a turning point in your ability to communicate openly. Blocks to logical thinking and effective writing are removed. And planet Neptune in your own sign of Capricorn till late November 1998 is unlocking keys to your subconscious and inner life. New challenges await you in the emotional realm. The new Saturn cycle gives you the opportunities to work on the feeling side of things.

Jupiter, planet of good fortune, is in your sign of Capricorn all 1996 to early 1997. Then Jupiter is in Aquarius, also a Saturn-ruled sign, 1997 to early 1998.

Jupiter's unexpected good luck here enables you to build on a solid base toward success. Jupiter is in Pisces 1998 to February 1999. Pisces, the water sign ruled by Neptune and co-ruled by Jupiter, is auspicious for Capricorn. The mix of water and earth, a natural medium for growth, can lead to fruitful alliances and artistic development. Meanwhile, Neptune in Capricorn gives creative expression form and focus.

New Uranus and Neptune cycles in the late '90s complement the expansive trend of Pluto in Sagittarius. Uranus, planet of innovation, leaves your sign of Capricorn in mid-January 1996 and enters Aquarius. Uranus in Aquarius 1996 to 2003 helps you let go of old constraints. It gives you the freedom to express emotional needs long pent up. Neptune, planet of visionary thought, enters Aquarius in late November 1998. Neptune in Aquarius 1998 to 2011 helps to remove Capricorn inhibitions so you can develop the intellectual and spiritual sides of your life. Formal studies and group associations play a large role as you travel and spread ideas in the professional and social arenas.

Jupiter in fiery Aries February 1999 to spring 2000 supplies boundless energy and reinforces self-reliance. And with Pluto in fiery Sagittarius you delve deep into your unconscious, tap into your private reserves of imagination and wisdom, let dreams lead you on a path of self-discovery. Although the journey may be painful at times, the rewards can be liberating if you summon the courage to participate fully. Jupiter in Aries gives you the daring and the courage to pursue those dreams.

Your planet Saturn starts a new cycle March 1999. Saturn enters Taurus for a three-year stay over the turn of the century. Taurus and Capricorn, both earth signs, are in good aspect to each other. Taurus brings love and money, and its steady influence keeps you from daredevil risks. With Saturn in Taurus into the year 2002 you can capitalize on golden opportunities and realize long-cherished dreams.

THE CUSP-BORN CAPRICORN

Are you *really* a Capricorn? If your birthday falls around Christmas, at the very beginning of Capricorn, will you still retain the traits of Sagittarius, the sign of the Zodiac before Capricorn? What if you were born during the 3rd week of January—are you more Aquarius than Capricorn? Many people born at the edge, or cusp, of a sign have great difficulty determining exactly what sign they are. If you are one of these people, here's how you can figure it out, once and for all.

Consult the table on page 17. Find the year of your birth, and then note the day. The table will tell you the precise days on which the Sun entered and left your sign. Whether you were born at the beginning or end of Capricorn, yours is a lifetime reflecting a process of subtle transformation. Your life on Earth will symbolize a significant change in consciousness, for you are either about to enter a whole new way of living, or you are leaving one behind.

If you were born at the beginning of Capricorn, you may want to read the horoscope book for Sagittarius as well as Capricorn, for Sagittarius is a deep—often hidden—part of your spirit. You were born with the special gift of being able to bring your dreams into reality and put your talents and ambitions to practical use.

You need to conquer worry and depression and learn to take life seriously, but without losing your sense of humor and hope. You must find a balance between believing nothing and believing too much. You need to find the firm middle ground between cynicism and idealism.

15

If you were born at the end of Capricorn, you may want to read the horoscope book on Aquarius, for you are a dynamic mixture of both the Capricorn and Aquarius natures.

You are in a transitional state of consciousness, about to enter a whole new way of living, but still dutybound to perform responsibilities before you are set free. You are bound by two lifestyles, one conservative, the other freedom-oriented. You combine the talents of regularity and discipline with rebellious spontaneity and flashing genius.

You can be troubled by reversals and setbacks, despite your serious planning, and find great conflict between personal ambitions and deep desires for freedom. You have a great pull toward the future, but you are powerfully drawn back to society and cultural conditioning.

THE CUSPS OF CAPRICORN

DATES SUN ENTERS CAPRICORN
(LEAVES SAGITTARIUS)

December 22 every year from 1900 to 2000,
except for the following:

December 21

1912	1944	1964	1977	1989
16	48	65	80	92
20	52	68	81	93
23	53	69	84	94
28	56	72	85	96
32	57	73	86	97
36	60	76	88	98
40	61			

DATES SUN LEAVES CAPRICORN
(ENTERS AQUARIUS)

January 20 every year from 1900 to 2000,
except for the following:

January 19		January 21		
1977	1989	1903	1920	1932
81	93	04	24	36
85	97	08	28	44
		12		

CAPRICORN RISING:
YOUR ASCENDANT

Could you be a "double" Capricorn? That is, could you have Capricorn as your Rising sign as well as your Sun sign? The tables on pages 20–21 will tell you Capricorns what your Rising sign happens to be. Just find the hour of your birth, then find the day of your birth, and you will see which sign of the Zodiac is your Ascendant, as the Rising sign is called. For a detailed discussion on how the Rising sign is determined, see pages 82–85.

Your Ascendant, or Rising sign, modifies your basic Sun sign personality, and it affects the way you act out the daily predictions for your Sun sign. If your Rising sign is indeed Capricorn, what follows is a description of its effects on your horoscope. If your Rising sign is some other sign of the Zodiac, you may wish to read the horoscope book for that sign.

With Capricorn Rising, look to beautiful planet Saturn, your ruler. Saturn makes you philosophical and wise, with a penchant for lone pursuits. You can see reality from many perspectives. And you are motivated to test the viability of each framework you discover. But you want to test life your own way, and be accountable only to yourself. Planet Saturn gives you a melancholy turn of mind.

You have an immense respect for the best order of things, for the way people should relate to each other in order to support each other. And you want to weave this order and support into the fabric of your own life and also into the larger tapestry of society as a whole. Your underlying drive is to integrate concepts of how people should behave with your self-concept. You start with a principle, then you expand it.

You have a remarkable ability to create far-reaching plans and to see them through. You can put kaleidoscopic images into focus. You can galvanize scattered energies into a powerful momentum. You are an excellent manager of people. You are happiest when you have unlimited responsibility to carry out such tasks. A family or a company is grist for your mill. Power to you means the ability to achieve your aims. Power is not fame, fortune, fondness, or any other measure of how people judge you. You are your own judge.

Capricorn Rising individuals are sensitive to the ways people treat your principles. In your mind your identity and your principles are merged. So when your ideas are insulted, you are insulted. You dislike rule breakers, and for that you may earn a reputation for sternness. You detest traitors, philanderers, cheats of all kinds. And for that you may be called rigid and old-fashioned. You consider a breach of trust and a lack of support dishonorable, because such behavior is harmful and hurtful. And you can be pitiless in your scorn for the perpetrator.

Your persona may be so identified with your principles that you restrain your impulses and suppress your emotions. You may refuse to let joy show even though you are probably the first one to see the humor in a situation. You will try to make your feelings fit your preconceptions instead of letting feelings build ideas. It is hard for you to tolerate contradiction and ambiguity. Only when emotion and idea match, can you relax and go with the flow.

The key words for Capricorn Rising are form and focus. Your own uphill struggle is a model of success for those who would despair and give in. Don't conserve your talents in seclusion. Connect on deep levels and help people build their lives.

RISING SIGNS FOR CAPRICORN

Hour of Birth	Day of Birth		
	December 21–26	December 27–31	January 1–5
Midnight	Virgo; Libra 12/22	Libra	Libra
1 AM	Libra	Libra	Libra
2 AM	Libra	Libra; Scorpio 12/29	Scorpio
3 AM	Scorpio	Scorpio	Scorpio
4 AM	Scorpio	Scorpio	Scorpio; Sagittarius 1/5
5 AM	Sagittarius	Sagittarius	Sagittarius
6 AM	Sagittarius	Sagittarius	Sagittarius
7 AM	Sagittarius	Capricorn	Capricorn
8 AM	Capricorn	Capricorn	Capricorn
9 AM	Capricorn; Aquarius 12/26	Aquarius	Aquarius
10 AM	Aquarius	Aquarius	Aquarius; Pisces 1/2
11 AM	Pisces	Pisces	Pisces
Noon	Pisces; Aries 12/22	Aries	Aries
1 PM	Aries; Taurus 12/26	Taurus	Taurus
2 PM	Taurus	Taurus	Gemini
3 PM	Gemini	Gemini	Gemini
4 PM	Gemini	Gemini	Cancer
5 PM	Cancer	Cancer	Cancer
6 PM	Cancer	Cancer	Cancer
7 PM	Cancer; Leo 12/22	Leo	Leo
8 PM	Leo	Leo	Leo
9 PM	Leo	Leo; Virgo 12/30	Virgo
10 PM	Virgo	Virgo	Virgo
11 PM	Virgo	Virgo	Virgo

	Day of Birth		
Hour of Birth	January 6–10	January 11–15	January 16–21
Midnight	Libra	Libra	Libra
1 AM	Libra	Libra; Scorpio 1/13	Libra
2 AM	Scorpio	Scorpio	Scorpio
3 AM	Scorpio	Scorpio	Scorpio; Sagittarius 1/21
4 AM	Sagittarius	Sagittarius	Sagittarius
5 AM	Sagittarius	Sagittarius	Sagittarius
6 AM	Sagittarius; Capricorn 1/7	Capricorn	Capricorn
7 AM	Capricorn	Capricorn	Capricorn
8 AM	Capricorn; Aquarius 1/7	Aquarius	Aquarius
9 AM	Aquarius	Aquarius	Aquarius; Pisces 1/17
10 AM	Pisces	Pisces	Pisces; Aries 1/21
11 AM	Aries	Aries	Aries
Noon	Aries; Taurus 1/10	Taurus	Taurus
1 PM	Taurus	Taurus; Gemini 1/15	Gemini
2 PM	Gemini	Gemini	Gemini
3 PM	Gemini	Gemini; Cancer 1/15	Cancer
4 PM	Cancer	Cancer	Cancer
5 PM	Cancer	Cancer	Cancer; Leo 1/21
6 PM	Leo	Leo	Leo
7 PM	Leo	Leo	Leo
8 PM	Leo	Leo; Virgo 1/14	Virgo
9 PM	Virgo	Virgo	Virgo
10 PM	Virgo	Virgo	Virgo; Libra 1/21
11 PM	Libra	Libra	Libra

LOVE AND RELATIONSHIPS

No matter who you are, what you do in life, or where your planets are positioned, you still need to be loved, and to feel love for other human beings. Human relationships are founded on many things: infatuation, passion, sex, guilt, friendship, and a variety of other complex motivations, frequently called love.

Relationships often start out full of hope and joy, the participants sure of themselves and sure of each other's love, and then end up more like a pair of gladiators than lovers. When we are disillusioned, bitter, and wounded, we tend to blame the other person for difficulties that were actually present long before we ever met. Without seeing clearly into our own natures we will be quite likely to repeat our mistakes the next time love comes our way.

Enter Astrology.

It is not always easy to accept, but knowledge of ourselves can improve our chances for personal happiness. It is not just by predicting when some loving person will walk into our lives, but by helping us come to grips with our failures and reinforce our successes.

Astrology won't solve all our problems. The escapist will ultimately have to come to terms with the real world around him. The hard-bitten materialist will eventually acknowledge the eternal rhythms of the infinite beyond which he can see or hear. Astrology does not merely explain away emotion. It helps us unify the head with the heart so that we can become whole individuals. It helps us define what it is we are searching for, so we can recognize it when we find it.

Major planetary cycles have been changing people's ideas about love and commitment, marriage, partnerships, and relationships. These cycles have affected virtually everyone in areas of personal involvement. Planetary forces point out upheavals and transformations occurring in all of society. The concept of marriage is being totally reexamined. Exactly what the changes will ultimately bring no one can tell. It is usually difficult to determine which direction society will take. One thing is certain: no man is an island. If the rituals and pomp of wedding ceremonies must be revised, then it will happen.

Social rules are being revised. Old outworn institutions are indeed crumbling. But relationships will not die. People are putting less stress on permanence and false feelings of security. The emphasis now shifts toward the union of two loving souls. Honesty, equality, and mutual cooperation are the goals in modern marriage. When these begin to break down, the marriage is in jeopardy. Surely there must be a balance between selfish separatism and prematurely giving up.

There is no doubt that astrology can establish the degree of compatibility between two human beings. Two people can share a common horizon in life but have quite different habits or basic interests. Two others might have many basic characteristics in common while needing to approach their goals from vastly dissimilar points of view. Astrology describes compatibility based on these assumptions.

It compares and contrasts through the fundamental characteristics that draw two people together. Although they could be at odds on many basic levels, two people could find themselves drawn together again and again. Sometimes it seems that we keep being attracted to the same type of individuals. We might ask ourselves if we have learned anything from our past mistakes. The answer is that there are qualities in people that we require and thus seek out time and time again. To solve that mystery in ourselves is to solve much of the dilemma of love, and so to help ourselves determine if we are approaching a wholesome situation or a potentially destructive one.

We are living in a very curious age with respect to marriage and relationships. We can easily observe the shifting social attitudes concerning the whole institution of marriage. People are seeking everywhere for answers to their own inner needs. In truth, all astrological combinations can achieve compatibility. But many relationships seem doomed before they get off the ground. Astrologically there can be too great a difference between the goals, aspirations, and personal outlook of the people involved. Analysis of both horoscopes must and will indicate enough major planetary factors to keep the two individuals together. Call it what you will: determination, patience, understanding, love—whatever it may be, two people have the capacity to achieve a state of fulfillment together. We all have different needs and desires. When it comes to choosing a mate, you really have to know yourself. If you know the truth about what you are really looking for, it will make it easier to find. Astrology is a useful, almost essential, tool to that end.

In the next chapter your basic compatibility with each of the twelve signs of the Zodiac is generalized. The planetary vibrations between you and an individual born under any given zodiacal sign suggest much about how you will relate to each other. Hints are provided about love and romance, sex and marriage so that you and your mate can get the most out of the relationship that occupies so important a role in your life.

CAPRICORN:
YOU AND YOUR MATE

CAPRICORN—ARIES

Aries creativity, zest, and super confidence can make a brilliant combination with Capricorn patience, method, and determination. Aries has the driving force and Capricorn has the way with people. Together you can accomplish the impossible. Of course, Aries will think it takes too long and Capricorn will think it's a little harebrained or crazy. But when you put your heads together to confer or conspire, the result is the successful execution of any Herculean task.

Tension will be great in such a relationship, since the fire of the Aries spirit must submit to the cool, earthy approach of Capricorn stability and practicality. The worried Capricorn's need for control will be upset by Aries' stubborn independence and refusal to knuckle under to facts. But understanding and a mutual desire for growth can prevent a frustrating stalemate, a deadlock that even time cannot solve.

You can weather professional battles, crisis situations, and romantic storms for the purpose of sharing your goals. You both need sustenance and security. Any burdens or responsibilities that circumstances impose on your lives can help you grow closer and more determined to succeed through loving each other.

Hints for Your Aries Mate

This alliance combines the Aries spontaneity of youthful aggression and the Capricorn caution of seasoned determination. Both of you want to get somewhere important. In the beginning you'll help each other and take advantage of your differences to score points against people and situations who would hold you back. As your relationship continues, you might have difficulty holding on to each other, as your very differences may be seen as holding each other back, too. You will automatically check your bank balance when Aries suggests new expenditures, and Aries is likely to suggest some wild and foolish ones. Aries will resent you for appearing skeptical. Try to be as charming with your Aries mate when you are alone together, doing your mutual bookkeeping, as you are in public, where your debonair attitude smooths the feathers Aries has ruffled. You need each other.

CAPRICORN—TAURUS

To thaw out a Capricorn, bring a Taurus around and watch the results. Slowly the ice melts and gradually the temperature rises. This is a blend that grows more compatible with time. You are both stubborn, cautious, and resistant to external change or control. But you look upon life in much the same way. Once you've established yourselves with the confidence of your own individual beings, you are warm and appreciative of one another.

Where your union may lack wild excitement, you provide depth of understanding, loyalty, and steadfast devotion. Where the two of you have been wild, uncontrollably passionate, or irresponsible, you will begin to feel maturity, security, and responsible faithfulness. Money and status will play a significant role in your union. Your position in the community will be crucial at some meaningful moment in your choices and decisions. You are the union of the need for luxury and the spartan capacity to sacrifice.

Together you can be the symbols of greed, ambition,

and lust to get ahead. You can be the picture of narrowness and fearful, penny-pinching gloom. But through love and cooperation, you can be the reflection of success through perseverence, determination, and your love for the beautiful things in life.

Hints for Your Taurus Mate

Here is one relationship where you don't have to be afraid to show your feelings. Your Taurus mate has the most wondrous way of making things feel all right, even when you are convinced the world is against you. Taurus does this naturally. But unless your mate begins to see some tangible rewards for his or her magic touch, he or she will just as magically wander off to more appreciative arms. And the rewards you bestow don't have to be all material ones. In fact, Taurus may suspect that you suspect he or she is a golddigger if you consistently show praise through things. Inspire the artist in your mate; after all, Taurus has some lovely natural talents which sometimes go unnoticed because they are not being used to make a living. Inspire your Taurus to sing, sew, dance, design, paint, potter; but be sure the effort is not connected with homemaking, or your mate will feel you're taking advantage. The best inspiration, of course, is lovemaking on all levels of expression.

CAPRICORN—GEMINI

If you want to make this relationship work, you will have to come to terms with the conflicts in your own nature. And if you have been drawn to Gemini, there are some mighty strong riddles to be solved. You have formed a strange union that pits depth and seriousness against restless curiosity—the need for security and stability against eternal craving for change. This may seem such a fundamental conflict that you give up and end the relationship before giving it a chance. But the conflict is within each of you.

You both require regularity, order, and discipline. But you both also have an equivocal, ambiguous streak that rejects the sober, thrifty, wise course of action in favor of reckless, trial-and-error superficiality. You both need the certainty of a life constructed out of honest hard work, method, and determination. At the same time, each of you is repelled by a plodding everyday life and cannot survive without versatility, mobility, and change.

In order to make anything lasting out of this relationship, you and your partner need to recognize the conflicts within yourselves, before solving the riddle of your relationship.

Hints for Your Gemini Mate

In this alliance, you and your Gemini mate will always be involved in high-powered situations because your Gemini mate thinks that way. The simplest thing can become an epic. Notwithstanding her or his logic, Gemini loves complications. You, who like to pursue the fabrics of life one thread at a time until they are raveled neatly or woven straightly, will be constantly startled and probably upset. Calm down. Gemini will never get you in trouble, and besides you'll never have a dull moment. If you do try to conserve your mate's talents for the unexpected or the bizarre, you will end up repressing them and her or him as well. That pall could spell the end of the affair. So be more tolerant, more alive to your Gemini lover's special way of loving you, of bringing you morsels of life into the livingroom to admire and engage. Get engaged; share your lover's dictum that variety is the spice of life.

CAPRICORN—CANCER

This is one of the best combinations in the whole Zodiac. You join emotional intimacy with worldly strength, the strong union of home life and business success. Provided you can accept your roles maturely, you have one of the strongest ties going. The natural process of long-term change will teach both of you a great deal about the potentials and pitfalls of such a combination.

Problems in your relationship usually occur when one of you plays the starving baby—insecure, misunderstood, and neglected. The other one plays the cold, unresponsive stepparent, the implacable and unyielding head of the orphanage. Such a Capricorn-Cancer relationship soon reaches a crisis stage—you either split up or grow up. Then when you assume your adult roles, accepting each other and yourselves, you can set about living your happy lives.

At worst, you can be uptight, status-seeking conformists, repressing every drive but the drive to get ahead. You can both be caught in a war between feelings of rejection and a cold, gloomy fear of love.

At best, you can encourage each other to succeed, and can grow more fully in the knowledge and security of each other's love. To respect each other's need for silence, introspection, and separateness is to accept each other's need for communion, fulfillment, and completion. The key is to transform yourselves into healthy adults, uniting the faculties of head and heart, feeling and reason.

Hints for Your Cancer Mate

Your natural reserves of patience and your natural reticence will get a good working out in this relationship with moody Cancer. Although you respect privacy, wanting it a great deal for yourself as well, you may begin to think that your Cancer mate carries his or her preoccupation with it to an extreme. Sometimes you will get the feeling that Cancer believes the world revolves around him or her alone. It won't do you any good to batter down the emotional gates, Goat that you are. Your Cancer lover's unyielding exterior is a resistant barrier. Yet do not be fooled into thinking your mate is not sensitive. Quite the contrary is true, and you can be the perfect lover if you keep that fact number one in your mind and number one in your behavior. While your mate is having a sulk, tend to the joint responsibilities of your union; don't let things go adrift. Cancer will want to come back to that cozy, loving nest.

CAPRICORN—LEO

At first you might think this is an unlikely combination, like moving a tropical island to the North Pole. But you two have many things in common, and can bring each other to greater growth, development, and maturity. You'll complain about Leo's constant demands— emotional and practical—and you'll meet problems that will be insurmountable to younger or immature members of your respective zodiacal signs.

You are both strong people who like to be in control of your lives. You dislike feeling that you're hardening, getting old or rusty or unattractive. You both like to feel in command of your emotions and are both concerned with the image (or spectacle) you're making of yourself. You're both ambitious, conservative animals imbued with the drive, determination, and stamina to get what you want.

When you don't get your own way, you both can get ugly. Yet you are both honorable, constant, and desirous of doing your best and being great at whatever you do. Capricorn makes Leo work and points out all the unfinished tasks that must be done in order for Leo to make it in the world. Leo turns Capricorn on, financially, professionally, or sexually, and the pair can do a lot together. This relationship reflects your need to unify the hot with the cold within yourself, to temper the passion of youth with the responsibility of a mature parent figure.

Hints for Your Leo Mate

Together you share one quality in common with your Leo mate that could either be a boon to the relationship or make it a bust. That is your unfailing honesty about calling things the way you see them. Both of you insist on telling the other things that might make another person blush or bolt. But fortunately both of you only do this in private; both you and Leo hate public scenes and would rather die than embarrass each other in front of other people. This candor, which you two have developed in the context of a loving relationship, is quite unusual. If you can keep it from causing friction with each other, your relationship will work. But sometimes neither one of you appreciates the bluntness or brutality. Now develop your basic charming way into a soothing facade for your Leo mate on those occasions when she or he feels really down, discouraged, ego-hurt. Leo needs pampering. Surely that won't discredit your honesty or wear out your endurance.

CAPRICORN—VIRGO

You are a truly harmonious pair. You may be critical of each other, but you can depend on each other for sound advice. However, don't make the mistake of invading each other's privacy or taking undue liberties.

You can develop your capacity to love and understand both yourselves and each other by the steady steps of trusting, helping, and being reasonable. Virgo loves with a deep, sincere affection that flows slowly with time, a solid emotion of steadfast, secure love. You will each know your responsibilities to each other and your loyalties will be called upon as long as your relationship lasts. You are both earnest, shy creatures, repelled by your own practicality, but able to accept each other because you feel so many of the same things.

Capricorn and Virgo together can be fearful of emotion. At worst, your fears make you petty and small, criticizing and disapproving, but cloaking your disdain in polite conversation. You can be narrow and prejudiced. Neither of you can bear being controlled by others, although you often feel you are, and you may not always express your fears candidly. You could talk a lot and not say what you feel. In time, no matter what, your love deepens and your trust grows.

But you can be honestly affectionate with each other, if a little distant. Virgo's presence in your life can offer invaluable help in philosophy, work, and career. Clarity of vision is your mutual strong point.

Hints for Your Virgo Mate

Perhaps no one can appreciate your solemn, saturnine qualities better than your Virgo mate. She or he will be able to read much humor and irony in what others may take only for a seasoned wisdom, dry of emotion and devoid of wit. That's why you are drawn to Virgo; Virgo truly appreciates the rich, varied underside of your emotional life, which few people get a chance to see, let alone experience. Don't treat your Virgo lover merely as the admiring critic, the aloof onlooker. Get in there and make Virgo experience his or her own deep underside, as well as vicariously enjoying yours. Here is someone shyer than you, more finicky than you, possibly even afraid. You have brain and brawn, so put them in the service of making your Virgo lover secure and ready to take a risk on serious lovemaking. The fringe benefits will be a wild abandon, a carefree excursion into mind and body both of you might not dare without the other.

CAPRICORN—LIBRA

Capricorn and Libra together form a serious combination of loyalty and stability. You provide each other with the homey security and driving ambition for career that both require. Either of you may be rebuffed and feel emotionally cheated at times, for the warmth that you feel you deserve is not always what you really need. But you're quite a pair—loyal, sturdy, and perfectly matched. Conservative and somewhat old-fashioned, you are status-conscious and often slightly insecure about your position.

The Capricorn-Libra combination can symbolize the union of beauty and practicality, and your home reflects it. When one of you is unresponsive, the other one goes crazy. When one of you is dreamy and unrealistic, there's trouble at home. Don't get caught in someone else's arms either. That's real trouble for the relationship.

In a relationship with Libra there will be great changes in the way you both approach business and social life. There will be transformations in both your personas, too. You are both more sharply aware of your ambitions and needs, as individuals and together. What keeps your relationship alive is a union of tact and determination. Of all the Capricorn pairings around the Zodiac, Capricorn-Libra can see each other through crises as nobody can.

Hints for Your Libra Mate

Being attractive to yourself, to your mate, and to other people who see you in a relationship is one of the great benefits of having a Libra lover. You will never doubt your attractiveness. Your native charm and way with people will get a big boost from Libra, who likes to show you off in company. You'll never have more friends, fanciers, hangers-on. You might get tired of it, feel a little boxed in, and begin to withdraw from Libra's gay world of sparkle, glitter, and glib conversation. That negative response could get you right out of the relationship, and you only intended to put a curfew on party time. So try, gallantly, to go along with the lovely social ideas of your Libra, even if you can't truly enjoy them. On the positive side, you can do much more. Build a big, broad base of success and wisdom from which your Libra mate can operate, and always be there to settle the controversies. Love is your main mutual asset.

CAPRICORN—SCORPIO

If you have developed a relationship based on mutual respect, you can be a source of strength to each other. You can be truly good friends—maybe better friends than lovers. Yours is a conflict between intensity and stability. At best you can be a turned-on couple with one eye open to reality. Sexually, this can be a powerful match, for the involvement is anything but light. You share a need for strong ties, and the depth of your involvement will always show that.

On the other hand, games of power and control are irresistible, for you both have strong wills and must feel that you are indispensable to your partner. You need acceptance, and must be loved, honored, and obeyed. When you go to war, your weapons will be totally different, and the war could last long on both sides. Neither of you is a total forgiver and forgetter.

Through loyalty and practicality your relationship is sure to deepen no matter how long it takes. And it will take time, for you are both hard to know. You are both able, courageous people and no struggle is too great for you to undertake. The older you get the tougher you get. Maturity brings new wisdom to your association.

You are a very powerful combination of sex and career drive, though sometimes you are more successful apart than you are together.

Hints for Your Scorpio Mate

You will certainly be regarded as an authority figure in this relationship, whether you are one or not. Your Scorpio mate may feel all bets are off. He or she may not even try to convince you, gall you, trick you, maneuver you. Temper, tantrum, tumult will be the name of the game; tactics have gone out the window. Well, at least you won't have to cope with your lover's slyness or sting; you'll have your hands full managing all the emotion. Maybe, though, that's the wrong way to respond to your Scorpio lover. Managing is not exactly what they want. They turn to you for the real response, the unguarded one, the spontaneous one. To you, it may seem a childish one, because all your life the unguarded response was the one you felt most likely to fail. That belief is probably the karma between you and Scorpio. If you are long on patience, you can get your lover out of their childishness and into your world. If you can't, no amount of good sex will keep you together.

CAPRICORN—SAGITTARIUS

If you get this act together in time, you'll be a smash hit on the planet Earth. The enthusiasm and casual resilience of Sagittarius combines well with the thoughtful planning and determined ambition of Capricorn. You bring Sagittarius down to earth when it comes to money. When you begin to build a financial reality out of your very real practical needs, your secret belief in luck starts paying off tangibly. Sagittarius, although often your undoing, broadens your scope and makes a fuller life possible.

At worst, your lives together may suffer from lack

of realism, depth, and determination and a painful in-consistency. You may bounce from a casual and care-less ease to a greedy search for concrete stability and security, from a stubborn decision to flout facts and enjoy yourself to the grim awakening of life's ironies.

But at best, you and Sagittarius together are the union of dreams and concrete reality. You can together embody wisdom, learning, and a true enrichment of mutual experience. You know how to enjoy yourselves and still face the responsibilities of your adult lives.

Hints for Your Sagittarius Mate

Sometimes in this relationship you will get the feeling that your Sagittarius mate sweet-talked you into some-thing. You're never quite sure what it is. If you go about the business of the relationship sternly, trying to organize the vague threads of emotional and economic commitment into a tight fabric of living, you'll be less sure as time goes on. Sagittarius probably did sweet-talk you because she or he liked you. That does not mean in any way that Sagittarius can be like you. For-get that identity of wills, of purpose right away. The only identity you two can have is in bed, and don't sell that short. You'll be much happier having your roman-tic sweetheart where it counts. Go on about the busi-ness of life by yourself. Don't push Sagittarius into your mode. On the positive side, try to be ultratolerant of your mate's meanderings and irresponsibilities. Sex-ual love and intellectual respect are what you two can have together.

CAPRICORN—CAPRICORN

You are a modest and socially reserved couple. You are the masters of diplomacy and protocol, dutiful and considerate, polite and restrained. You are the proto-types of good breeding, no matter what your origins.

Your affection for each other will be genuine, no matter what sort of relationship you are involved in. You respect each other's privacy and can help each other in your careers or in dealing with some major obstacle that keeps you from achieving your ends.

Your relationship will grow into fruitfulness through a shared responsibility or burden, a circumstance that you both can use to build happy, useful lives.

You should be on your guard against gloom and neurotic fear. Avoid miserliness and cynicism, for you could use them to freeze each other out.

Though you are not wildly demonstrative, your understated devotion to each other is inspiring to others. Your love is deep, sincere, honest—built upon unshakable foundations of loyalty and trust. You understand each other's struggles in a total way.

Hints for Your Capricorn Mate

You two are probably secretly celebrating your togetherness, complimenting each other on having chosen so wisely, yet wondering all the while what other astrological configurations exist in your individual makeups that make you seem so different from one another. Who ever said that Capricorn is a one-dimensional creature? Besides, your curiosity together is probably the glue that cements you. You both could have a grand and satisfying time with each other, coming home at the end of the day to share your trials and tribulations, without need of company. Yet beware! That set between you could become so rigid you both lose your feel for real life if it is not reflected between the two of you. Which one of you will change first and abandon the other? Change together. Build a room onto your house every year, not just to look out of but to invite other people into. In that way, you'll have a lot more to mirror back and forth without abandoning each other.

CAPRICORN—AQUARIUS

You're an interesting pair because you can be very close while still being so deeply different. Together both of you feel the need to be shy and reserved, and yet long to be explosively spontaneous. Neither of you enjoys being bombed out of your reserved self, but you don't like your desires curtailed by any controlling forces.

Capricorn and Aquarius together can be torn between rigid discipline and chaotic disruption, caught by conflicts between your ambitions and your sense of independence. Each of you must accept and respect the other's need for privacy, independence, and security.

For this relationship to develop properly, you must give your Aquarius freedom and ask for support in return. You both desire liberation from life's limiting routines, and method is your greatest tool to that end. The relationship is complex, to say the least.

At best, you and Aquarius are the union of reason and genius, the symbol of the orderly transition from the old to the new.

Hints for Your Aquarius Mate

In this relationship you are reminded to rely on the planet that you and your Aquarius mate share: Saturn. Chances are you two got together in the first place because in that crowded room of crazy people each of you recognized a kindred soul—each other. Your gift for organizing information and Aquarius' gift for circulating information exchanged. Zip—you got together. You both may still do that, and it eases your relationship enormously. But every now and then you get the feeling that if you had been seeing more clearly, you would have seen your Aquarius also to be a little crazy. How come your lover is so unpredictable yet gloomy, so flagrant yet afraid, so scattered yet certain?

In the large view of things, obviously Uranus, the co-ruling planet of Aquarius, is messing things up. So bring the big gun, the planet Saturn, to the rescue. Show your Aquarius how to overcome the contradictions in personality. But let him or her show you the radical side of lovemaking and sexual excitement.

CAPRICORN—PISCES

Both Capricorn and Pisces combine hardheaded pragmatism and idle dreaminess. Each of you has that individual riddle to solve, and must come to terms with yourself if you are to be happy together.

Basically, you are a harmonious pair, happy in silent company, coming together and parting. You need to respect the tides of your separate lives, for together you are like high seas crashing against the rocks in passionate thunder, leaving again when the tide goes out.

Your conflict is between concrete facts and vague abstract theories, between reason and emotion, the belief that life is made up of hard and tough realities that must be faced and the passive belief that everything is illusion and nothing really matters. The greatest danger to your relationship is that you will become involved in a silent, agonizing war between everyday reality and wishful poetry. It is important to develop the capacity to accept within yourselves the strange phobias and conflicts between head and heart that are part of both of you.

Together you can find a balance between believing nothing and believing too much. Once you learn to avoid fearful separatism and melting together in weak dependency, you add deep dimensions to each other's lives, through the totality of emotional contact and through the counsel of reason.

Hints for Your Pisces Mate

Hard cane sugar is what you and your Pisces lover can crop if you're sensible about it. Don't let that moon-light-and-molasses look fool you. Pisces is not all that sultry, and certainly not that lazy. Pisces is not dew, but the sea. And there's always a cold, biting chop to an ocean current riding on top of the waves. So it is with your relationship. Don't waste a lot of time trying to get your Pisces mate in line. And don't insult or mock their particular form of discipline. Do your own thing. But keep attuned for that special sound—a dim, rhythmic echo of earth pounding on earth by waves. Your own sound maybe? If you want structure, go back to the fields and harvest cane sugar together. If you want freedom, listen to your Pisces mate's dreams— don't scoff—and go where earth can regenerate. Your union is essentially sexual and melodramatic, so make the most of it.

CAPRICORN:
YOUR PROGRESSED SUN

WHAT IS YOUR NEW SIGN?

Your birth sign, or Sun sign, is the central core of your whole personality. It symbolizes everything you try to do and be. It is your main streak, your major source of power, vitality, and life. But as you live you learn, and as you learn you progress. The element in your horoscope that measures your progress is called the Progressed Sun. It is the symbol of your growth on Earth, and represents new threads that run through your life. The Progressed Sun measures big changes, turning points, and major decisions. It will often describe the path you are taking toward the fulfillment of your desires.

Below you will find brief descriptions of the Progressed Sun in three signs. According to the table on page 43, find out about your Progressed Sun and see how and where you fit into the cosmic scheme. Each period lasts about 30 years, so watch and see how dramatic these changes turn out to be.

If Your Sun Is Progressing Into—

AQUARIUS, you'll be wanting freedom from the restrictions of the past years. You will want to break new territory, throw off limitations, start fresh, and experiment with new things and new people. You will have contact with groups, societies, and friends. This is a time for advancement and putting past reversals into perspective.

PISCES, a spiritual need for reconciling failure with success is necessary. Guilt, disappointment, and sorrow are illusions that must be pierced, for beyond them lies redemption. If you are plagued by doubts, anxieties, or uncertainties, be assured that success and happiness will come through devotion, faith, compassion, forgiveness, and love.

ARIES, you start gathering a sense of who you are and a basic zest and enthusiasm for life. You speak up for yourself and become more open and honest. You'll feel more aggressive and will respond to challenges more readily. You may even look for challenge. You are experiencing an awakening of self.

HOW TO USE THE TABLE

Look for your birthday in the table on the facing page. Then, under the appropriate column, find out approximately when your Progressed Sun will lead you to a new sign. From that point on, for 30 years, the thread of your life will run through that sign. Read the definitions on the preceding pages and see exactly how that life thread will develop.

For example, if your birthday is December 31, your Progressed Sun will enter Aquarius around your 21st birthday and will travel through Aquarius until you are 51 years old. Your Progressed Sun will then move into Pisces. Reading the definitions of Aquarius and Pisces will tell you much about your major involvements and interests during those years.

YOUR PROGRESSED SUN

If your birthday falls on:	start looking at AQUARIUS at age	start looking at PISCES at age	start looking at ARIES at age
Dec. 22	30	60	90
23	29	59	89
24	28	58	88
25	27	57	87
26	26	56	86
27	25	55	85
38	24	54	84
29	23	53	83
30	22	52	82
31	21	51	81
January 1	20	50	80
2	19	49	79
3	18	48	78
4	17	47	77
5	16	46	76
6	15	45	75
7	14	44	74
8	13	43	73
9	12	42	72
10	11	41	71
11	10	40	70
12	9	39	69
13	8	38	68
14	7	37	67
15	6	36	66
16	5	35	65
17	4	34	64
18	3	33	63
19	2	32	62
20	1	31	61

CAPRICORN BIRTHDAYS

Dec. 21 Chris Evert, Jane Fonda
Dec. 22 E. A. Robinson, Lady Bird Johnson
Dec. 23 Jose Greco
Dec. 24 Howard Hughes, Ava Gardner
Dec. 25 Clara Barton, Little Richard
Dec. 26 Mao, Steve Allen
Dec. 27 Marlene Dietrich, Pasteur
Dec. 28 Woodrow Wilson, Maggie Smith
Dec. 29 Pablo Casals, Mary Tyler Moore
Dec. 30 Kipling, Bo Diddley
Dec. 31 Henri Matisse, Odetta
Jan. 1 Betsy Ross, Herbert Hoover, Xavier Cugat
Jan. 2 Stalin, Isaac Asimov, Renata Tebaldi
Jan. 3 Lucretia Mott, Zasu Pitts, Ray Milland
Jan. 4 Newton, Jacob Grimm
Jan. 5 Konrad Adenauer, Yogananda
Jan. 6 St. Joan, Tom Mix, Alan Watts
Jan. 7 Charles Addams, Emma Nevada
Jan. 8 Elvis Presley, Frances Workman
Jan. 9 Nixon, Gypsy Rose Lee, Joan Baez
Jan. 10 Ray Bolger, Galina Ulanova
Jan. 11 Eva le Gallienne, William James
Jan. 12 Vivekananda, Joe Frazier, Texas Guinan
Jan. 13 Horatio Alger
Jan. 14 Albert Schweitzer, Faye Dunaway
Jan. 15 Onassis, Nasser, Margaret O'Brien
Jan. 16 Ethel Merman, Eartha Kitt
Jan. 17 Ben Franklin, Al Capone
Jan. 18 Cezanne, Janis Joplin, Poe, Robert E. Lee
Jan. 19 Desi Arnaz, George Burns
Jan. 20 Federico Fellini, Pat Neal

CAN ASTROLOGY PREDICT THE FUTURE?

Can astrology really peer into the future? By studying the planets and the stars is it possible to look years ahead and make predictions for our lives? How can we draw the line between ignorant superstition and cosmic mystery? We live in a very civilized world, to be sure. We consider ourselves modern, enlightened individuals. Yet few of us can resist the temptation to take a peek at the future when we think it's possible. Why? What is the basis of such universal curiosity?

The answer is simple. Astrology works, and you don't have to be a magician to find that out. We certainly can't prove astrology simply by taking a look at the astonishing number of people who believe in it, but such figures do make us wonder what lies behind such widespread popularity. Everywhere in the world hundreds of thousands of serious, intelligent people are charting, studying, and interpreting the positions of the planets and stars every day. Every facet of the media dispenses daily astrological bulletins to millions of curious seekers. In Eastern countries, the source of many wisdoms handed down to us from antiquity, astrology still has a vital place. Why? Surrounded as we are by sophisticated scientific method, how does astrology, with all its bizarre symbolism and mysterious meaning, survive so magnificently? The answer remains the same. It works.

Nobody knows exactly where astrological knowledge came from. We have references to it dating back to the dawn of human history. Wherever there was a stirring of human consciousness, people began to observe the natural cycles and rhythms that sustained their life. The diversity of human behavior must have been evident even to the first students of consciousness. Yet the basic similarity between members of the human family must have led to the search for some common source, some greater point of origin somehow linked to the heavenly bodies ruling our sense of life and time. The ancient world of Mesopotamia, Chaldea, and Egypt was a highly developed center of astronomical observation and astrological interpretation of heavenly phenomena and their resultant effects on human life.

Amid the seeming chaos of a mysterious unknown universe, people from earliest times sought to classify, define, and organize the world around them. Order: that's what the human mind has always striven to maintain in an unceasing battle with its natural counterpart, chaos, or entropy. We build cities, countries, and empires, subjugating nature to a point of near defeat, and then . . . civilization collapses, empires fall, and cities crumble. Nature reclaims the wilderness. Shelly's poem *Ozymandias* is a hymn to the battle between order and chaos. The narrator tells us about a statue, broken, shattered, and half-sunk somewhere in the middle of a distant desert. The inscription reads: "Look on my works, ye mighty, and despair." And then we are told: "Nothing beside remains. Round the decay of that colossal wreck, boundless and bare, the lone and level sands stretch far away."

People always feared the entropy that seemed to lurk in nature. So we found permanence and constancy in the regular movements of the Sun, Moon, and planets and in the positions of the stars. Traditions sprang up from observations of the seasons and crops. Relationships were noted between phenomena in nature and the configurations of the heavenly bodies. This "synchronicity," as it was later called by Carl Jung, extended to thought, mood, and behavior, and as such developed the astrological archetypes handed down to us today.

Astrology, a regal science of the stars in the old days, was made available to the king, who was informed of impending events in the heavens, translated of course to their earthly meanings by trusted astrologers. True, astrological knowledge in its infant stages was rudimentary and beset with many superstitions and false premises. But those same dangers exist today in any investigation of occult or mystical subjects. In the East, reverence for astrology is part of religion. Astrologer-astronomers have held respected positions in government and have taken part in advisory councils on many momentous issues. The duties of the court astrologer, whose office was one of the most important in the land, were clearly defined, as early records show.

Here in our sleek Western world, astrology glimmers on, perhaps more brilliantly than ever. With all of our technological wonders and complex urbanized environments, we look to astrology even now to cut through artificiality, dehumanization, and all the materialism of contemporary life, while we gather precious information that helps us live in that material world. Astrology helps us restore balance and get in step with our own rhythms and the rhythms of nature.

Intelligent investigation of astrology (or the practical application of it) need not mean blind acceptance. We only need to see it working, see our own lives confirming its principles every day, in order to accept and understand it more. To understand ourselves is to know ourselves and to know all. This book can help you to do that—to understand yourself and through understanding develop your own resources and potentials as a rich human being.

YOUR PLACE AMONG THE STARS

Humanity finds itself at the center of a vast personal universe that extends infinitely outward in all directions. In that sense each is a kind of star radiating, as our Sun does, to all bodies everywhere. These vibrations, whether loving, helpful, or destructive, extend outward and generate a kind of "atmosphere" in which woman and man move. The way we relate to everything around us—our joy or our sorrow—becomes a living part of us. Our loved ones and our enemies become the objects of our projected radiations, for better or worse. Our bodies and faces reflect thoughts and emotions much the way light from the Sun reflects the massive reactions occurring deep within its interior. This energy and light reach all who enter its sphere of influence.

Our own personal radiations are just as potent in their own way, really. The reactions that go on deep within us profoundly affect our way of thinking and acting. Our feelings of joy or satisfaction, frustration or anger, must eventually find an outlet. Otherwise we experience the psychological or physiological repercussions of repression. If we can't have a good cry, tell someone our troubles, or express love, we soon feel very bad indeed.

As far as our physical selves are concerned, there is a direct relationship between our outer lives, inner reactions and actions, and the effects on our physical body. We all know the feeling of being startled by the sudden ring of a telephone, or the simple frustration of missing a bus. In fact, our minds and bodies are constantly reacting to outside forces. At the same time we, too, are generating actions that will cause a reaction in someone else. You may suddenly decide to phone a friend. If you are a bus driver you might speed along on your way and leave behind an angry would-be passenger. Whatever the case, mind and body are in close communication and they both reflect each other's condition. Next time you're really angry take a good long look in the mirror!

In terms of human evolution, our ability to understand, control, and ultimately change ourselves will naturally affect all of our outside relationships. Astrology is invaluable to helping us comprehend our inner selves. It is a useful tool in helping us retain our integrity, while cooperating with and living in a world full of other human beings.

Let's go back to our original question: Can astrology predict the future? To know that, we must come to an understanding of what the future is.

In simplest terms the future is the natural next step to the present, just as the present is a natural progression from the past. Although our minds can move from one to the other, there is a thread of continuity between past, present, and future that joins them together in a coherent sequence. If you are reading this book at this moment, it is the result of a real conscious choice you made in the recent past. That is, you chose to find out what was on these pages, picked up the book, and opened it. Because of this choice you may know yourself better in the future. It's as simple as that.

Knowing ourselves is the key to being able to predict and understand our own future. To learn from past experiences, choices, and actions is to fully grasp the present. Coming to grips with the present is to be master of the future.

"Know thyself" is a motto that takes us back to the philosophers of ancient Greece. Mystery religions and cults of initiation throughout the ancient world, schools of mystical discipline, yoga and mental expansion have always been guardians of this one sacred phrase. Know thyself. Of course, that's easy to say. But how do you go about it when there are so many conflicts in our lives and different parts of our personalities? How do we know when we are really "being ourselves" and not merely being influenced by the things we read or see on television, or by the people around us? How can we differentiate the various parts of our character and still remain whole?

There are many methods of classifying human beings into types. Body shapes, muscular types, blood types, and genetic types are only a few. Psychology has its own ways of classifying human beings according to their behavior. Anthropology studies human evolution as the body-mind response to environment. Biology watches physical development and adaptations in body structure. These fields provide valuable information about human beings and the ways they survive, grow, and change in their search for their place in eternity. Yet these branches of science have been separate and fragmented. Their contribution has been to provide theories and data, yes, but no lasting solutions to the human problems that have existed since the first two creatures realized they had two separate identities.

It's often difficult to classify yourself according to these different schemes. It's not easy to be objective about yourself. Some things are hard to face; others are hard to see. The different perspectives afforded to us by studying the human organism from all these different disciplines may seem contradictory when they are all really trying to integrate humankind into the whole of the cosmic scheme.

Astrology can help these disciplines unite to seek a broader and deeper approach to universal human issues. Astrology's point of view is vast. It transcends racial, ethnic, genetic, environmental, and even historical criteria, yet somehow includes them all. Astrology embraces the totality of human experience, then sets about to examine the relationships that are created within that experience.

We don't simply say, "The planets cause this or that." Rather than merely isolating cause or effect, astrology has unified the ideas of cause and effect. Concepts of past, present, and future merge and become, as we shall see a little later on, like stepping-stones across the great stream of mind. Observations of people and the environment have developed the astrological principles of planetary "influence," but it must be remembered that if there is actual influence, it is mutual. As the planets influence us, so we influence them, for we are forever joined to all past and future motion of the heavenly bodies. This is the foundation of astrology as it has been built up over the centuries.

ORDER VS. CHAOS

But is it all written in the stars? Is it destined that empires should thrive and flourish, kings reign, lovers love, and then . . . decay, ruin, and natural disintegration hold sway? Have we anything to do with determining the cycles of order and chaos? The art of the true astrologer depends on his ability to uncover new information, place it upon the grid of data already collected, and then interpret what he sees as accurate probability in human existence. There may be a paradox here. If we can predict that birds will fly south, could we not, with enough time and samples for observation, determine their ultimate fate when they arrive in the south?

The paradox is that there is no paradox at all. Order and chaos exist together simultaneously in one observable universe. At some remote point in time and space the Earth was formed, and for one reason or another, life appeared here. Whether the appearance of life on planets is a usual phenomenon or an unrepeated accident we can only speculate at this moment. But our Earth and all living things upon its surface conform to certain laws of physical materiality that our observations have led us to write down and contemplate. All creatures, from the one-celled ameba to a man hurrying home at rush hour, have some basic traits in common. Life in its organization goes from the simple to the complex with a perfection and order that is both awesome and inspiring. If there were no order to our physical world, an apple could turn into a worm and cows could be butterflies.

But the world is an integrated whole, unified with every other part of creation. When nature does take an unexpected turn, we call that a mutation. This is the exciting card in the program of living experience that tells us not everything is written at all. Spontaneity is real. Change is real. Freedom from the expected norm is real. We have seen in nature that only those mutations that can adapt to changes in their environment and continue reproducing themselves will survive. But possibilities are open for sudden transformation, and that keeps the whole world growing.

FREE CHOICE AND
THE VALUE OF PREDICTIONS

Now it's time to turn our attention to the matter of predictions. That was our original question after all: Can astrology peer into the future? Well, astrological prognostication is an awe-inspiring art and requires deep philosophical consideration before it is to be undertaken. Not only are there many grids that must be laid one upon the other before such predictions can be made, but there are ethical issues that plague every student of the stars. How much can you really see? How much should you tell? What is the difference between revealing valuable data and disclosing negative or harmful programing?

If an astrologer tells you only the good things, you'll have little confidence in the analysis when you are passing through crisis. On the other hand, if the astrologer is a prophet of doom who can see nothing but the dark clouds on the horizon, you will eventually have to reject astrology because you will come to associate it with the bad luck in your life.

Astrology itself is beyond any practitioner's capacity to grasp it all. Unrealistic utopianism or gloomy determinism reflect not the truth of astrology but the truth of the astrologer interpreting what he sees. In order to solve problems and make accurate predictions, you have to be *able* to look on the dark side of things without dwelling there. You have to be able to take a look at all the possibilities, all the possible meanings of a certain planetary influence without jumping to premature conclusions. Objective scanning and assessment take much practice and great skill.

No matter how skilled the astrologer is, he cannot assume the responsibility for your life. Only you can take that responsibility as your life unfolds. In a way, the predictions of this book are glancing ahead up the road, much the way a road map can indicate turns up ahead this way or that. You, however, are still driving the car.

What, then, is a horoscope? If it is a picture of you at your moment of birth, are you then frozen forever in time and space, unable to budge or deviate from the harsh, unyielding declarations of the stars? Not at all.

The universe is always in motion. Each moment follows the moment before it. As the present is the result of all past choices and action, so the future is the result of today's choices. But if we can go to a planetary calendar and see where planets will be located two years from now, then how can individual free choice exist? This is a question that has haunted authors and philosophers since the first thinkers recorded their thoughts. In the end, of course, we must all reason things out for ourselves and come to our own conclusions. It is easy to be impressed or influenced by people who seem to know a lot more than we do, but in reality we must all find codes of beliefs with which we are the most comfortable.

But if we can stretch our imaginations up, up above the line of time as it exists from one point to another, we can almost see past, present, and future, all together. We can almost feel this vibrant thread of creative free choice that pushes forward at every moment, actually causing the future to happen! Free will, that force that changes the entire course of a stream, exists within the stream of mind itself—the collective mind, or intelligence, of humanity. Past, present, and future are mere stepping-stones across that great current.

Our lives continue a thread of an intelligent mind

that existed before we were born and will exist after we die. It is like an endless relay race. At birth we pick up a torch and carry it, lighting the way with that miraculous light of consciousness of immortality. Then we pass it on to others when we die. What we call the *unconscious* may be part of this great stream of mind, which learns and shares experiences with everything that has ever lived or will ever live on this world or any other.

Yet we all come to Earth with different family circumstances, backgrounds, and characteristics. We all come to life with different planetary configurations. Indeed each person *is* different, yet we are all the same. We have different tasks or responsibilities or lifestyles, but underneath we share a common current—the powerful stream of human intelligence. Each of us has different sets of circumstances to deal with because of the choices he or she has made in the past. We all possess different assets and have different resources to fall back on, weaknesses to strengthen, and sides of our nature to transform. We are all what we are now because of what we were before. The present is the sum of the past. And we will be what we will be in the future because of what we are now.

It is foolish to pretend that there are no specific boundaries or limitations to any of our particular lives. Family background, racial, cultural, or religious indoctrinations, physical characteristics, these are all inescapable facts of our being that must be incorporated and accepted into our maturing mind. But each person possesses the capacity for breakthrough, forgiveness, and total transformation. It has taken millions of years since people first began to walk upright. We cannot expect an overnight evolution to take place. There are many things about our personalities that are very much like our parents. Sometimes that thought makes us uncomfortable, but it's true.

It's also true that we are not our parents. You are

you, just you, and nobody else but you. That's one of the wondrous aspects of astrology. The levels on which each planetary configuration works out will vary from individual to individual. Often an aspect of selfishness will be manifested in one person, yet in another it may appear as sacrifice and kindness.

Development is inevitable in human consciousness. But the direction of that development is not. As plants will bend toward the light as they grow, so there is the possibility for the human mind to grow toward the light of integrity and truth. The Age of Aquarius that everyone is talking about must first take place within each human's mind and heart. An era of peace, freedom, and community cannot be legislated by any government, no matter how liberal. It has to be a spontaneous flow of human spirit and fellowship. It will be a magnificent dawning on the globe of consciousness that reflects the joy of the human heart to be part of the great stream of intelligence and love. It must be generated by an enlightened, realistic humanity. There's no law that can put it into effect, no magic potion to drink that will make it all come true. It will be the result of all people's efforts to assume their personal and social responsibilities and to carve out a new destiny for humankind.

As you read the predictions in this book, bear in mind that they have been calculated by means of planetary positions for whole groups of people. Thus their value lies in your ability to coordinate what you read with the nature of your life's circumstances at the present time. You have seen how many complex relationships must be analyzed in individual horoscopes before sensible accurate conclusions can be drawn. No matter what the indications, a person has his or her own life, own intelligence, basic native strength that must ultimately be the source of action and purpose. When you are living truthfully and in harmony with what you know is right, there are no forces, threats, or obstacles that can defeat you.

With these predictions, read the overall pattern and see how rhythms begin to emerge. They are not caused by remote alien forces, millions of miles out in space. You and the planets are one. What you do, they do. What they do, you do. But can you change their course? No, but you cannot change many of your basic characteristics either. Still, within that already existing framework, you are the master. You can still differentiate between what is right for you and what is not. You can seize opportunities and act on them, you can create beauty and seek love.

The purpose of looking ahead is not to scare yourself. Look ahead to enlarge your perspective, enhance your overall view of the life *you* are developing. Difficult periods cause stress certainly, but at the same time they give you the chance to reassess your condition, restate and redefine exactly what is important to you, so you can cherish your life more. Joyous periods should be lived to the fullest with the happiness and exuberance that each person richly deserves.

YOUR HOROSCOPE AND THE ZODIAC

It's possible that in your own body, as you read this passage, there exist atoms as old as time itself. You could well be the proud possessor of some carbon and hydrogen (two necessary elements in the development of life) that came into being in the heart of a star billions and billions of years ago. That star could have exploded and cast its matter far into space. This matter could have formed another star, and then another, until finally our Sun was born. From the Sun's nuclear reactions came the material that later formed the planets—and maybe some of that primeval carbon or hydrogen. That material could have become part of the Earth, part of an early ocean, even early life. These same atoms could well have been carried down to the present day, to this very moment as you read this book. It's really quite possible. You can see how everything is linked to everything else. Our Earth now exists in a gigantic universe that showers it constantly with rays and invisible particles. You are the point into which all these energies and influences have been focused. You are the prism through which all the light of outer space is being refracted. You are literally a reflection of all the planets and stars.

Your horoscope is a picture of the sky at the moment of your birth. It's like a gigantic snapshot of the positions of the planets and stars, taken from Earth. Of course, the planets never stop moving around the Sun even for the briefest moment, and you represent that motion as it was occurring at the exact hour of your birth at the precise location on the Earth where you were born.

When an astrologer is going to read your chart, he or she asks you for the month, day, and year of your birth. She also needs the exact time and place. With this information he sets about consulting various charts and tables in his calculation of the specific positions of the Sun, Moon, and stars, relative to your birthplace when you came to Earth. Then he or she locates them by means of the *Zodiac*.

The Zodiac is a group of stars, centered against the Sun's apparent path around the Earth, and these star groups are divided into twelve equal segments, or *signs*. What we are actually dividing up is the Earth's path around the Sun. But from our point of view here on Earth, it seems as if the Sun is making a great circle around our planet in the sky, so we say it's the Sun's apparent path. This twelvefold division, the Zodiac, is like a mammoth address system for any body in the sky. At any given moment, the planets can all be located at a specific point along this path.

Now where are you in this system? First you look to your *Sun sign*—the section of the Zodiac that the Sun occupied when you were born. A great part of your character, in fact the central thread of your whole being, is described by your Sun sign. Each sign of the Zodiac has certain basic traits associated with it. Since the Sun remains in each sign for about thirty days, that divides the population into twelve major character types. Of course, not everybody born the same month will have the same character, but you'll be amazed at how many fundamental traits you share with your astrological cousins of the same birth sign, no matter how many environmental differences you boast.

The dates on which the Sun sign changes will vary from year to year. That is why some people born near the *cusp*, or edge, of a sign have difficulty determining their true birth sign without the aid of an astrologer who can plot precisely the Sun's apparent motion (the Earth's motion) for any given year. But to help you find your true Sun sign, a Table of Cusp Dates for the years 1900 to 2000 is provided for you on page 17.

Here are the twelve signs of the Zodiac as western astrology has recorded them. Listed also are the symbols associated with them and the *approximate* dates when the Sun enters and exits each sign for the year 1999.

Aries	Ram	March 20–April 20
Taurus	Bull	April 20–May 21
Gemini	Twins	May 21–June 21
Cancer	Crab	June 21–July 23
Leo	Lion	July 23–August 23
Virgo	Virgin	August 23–September 23
Libra	Scales	September 23–October 23
Scorpio	Scorpion	October 23–November 22
Sagittarius	Archer	November 22–December 22
Capricorn	Sea Goat	December 22–January 20
Aquarius	Water Bearer	January 20–February 18
Pisces	Fish	February 18-March 20

In a horoscope the *Rising sign*, or Ascendant, is often considered to be as important as the Sun sign. In a later chapter (see pages 82–84) the Rising sign is discussed in detail. But to help you determine your own Rising sign, a Table of Rising Signs is provided for you on pages 20–21.

THE SIGNS OF THE ZODIAC

The signs of the Zodiac are an ingenious and complex summary of human behavioral and physical types, handed down from generation to generation through the bodies of all people in their hereditary material and through their minds. On the following pages you will find brief descriptions of all twelve signs in their highest and most ideal expression.

ARIES
The Sign of the Ram

Aries is the first sign of the Zodiac, and marks the beginning of springtime and the birth of the year. In spring the Earth begins its ascent upward and tips its North Pole toward the Sun. During this time the life-giving force of the Sun streams toward Earth, bathing our planet with the kiss of warmth and life. Plants start growing. Life wakes up. No more waiting. No more patience. The message has come from the Sun: Time to live!

Aries is the sign of the Self and is the crusade for the right of an individual to live in unimpeachable freedom. It represents the supremacy of the human will over all obstacles, limitations, and threats. In Aries there is unlimited energy, optimism, and daring, for it is the pioneer in search of a new world. It is the story of success and renewal, championship, and victory. It is the living spirit of resilience and the power to be yourself, free from all restrictions and conditioning. There is no pattern you *have* to repeat, nobody's rule you *have* to follow.

Confidence and positive action are born in Aries, with little thought or fear of the past. Life is as magic as sunrise, with all the creative potential ahead of you for a new day. Activity, energy, and adventure characterize this sign. In this sector of the Zodiac there is amazing strength, forthrightness, honesty, and a stubborn refusal to accept defeat. The Aries nature is forgiving, persuasive, masterful, and decisive.

In short, Aries is the magic spark of life and being, the source of all initiative, courage, independence, and self-esteem.

TAURUS
The Sign of the Bull

Taurus is wealth. It is not just money, property, and the richness of material possessions, but also a wealth of the spirit. Taurus rules everything in the visible world we see, touch, hear, smell, taste—the Earth, sea, and sky—everything we normally consider "real." It is the sign of economy and reserve, for it is a mixture of thrift and luxury, generosity and practicality. It is a blend of the spiritual and material, for the fertility of the sign is unlimited, and in this sense it is the mystical bank of life. Yet it must hold the fruit of its efforts in its hands and seeks to realize its fantasy-rich imagination with tangible rewards.

Loyalty and endurance make this sign perhaps the most stable of all. We can lean on Taurus, count on it,

and it makes our earthly lives comfortable, safe, pleasurable. It is warm, sensitive, loving, and capable of
magnificent, joyful sensations. It is conservative and
pragmatic, with a need to be sure of each step forward.
It is the capacity to plan around eventualities without
living in the future. Steadfast and constant, this is a
sturdy combination of ruggedness and beauty, gentleness and unshakability of purpose. It is the point at
which we join body and soul. Unselfish friend and loyal
companion, Taurus is profoundly noble and openly humanitarian. Tenacity and concentration slow the energy down to bring certain long-lasting rewards.

Taurus is a fertile resource and rich ground to grow in,
and we all need it for our ideas and plans to flourish. It is
the uncut diamond, symbolizing rich, raw tastes and a
deep need for satisfaction, refinement, and completion.

GEMINI
The Sign of the Twins

Gemini is the sign of mental brilliance. Communication
is developed to a high degree of fluidity, rapidity, fluency.
It is the chance for expressing ideas and relaying information from one place to another. Charming, debonair,
and lighthearted, it is a symbol of universal interest and
eternal curiosity. The mind is quick and advanced, with a
lightning-like ability to assimilate data.

It is the successful manipulation of verbal or visual
language and the capacity to meet all events with ob-
jectivity and intelligence. It is light, quick wit, with a
comic satiric twist. Gemini is the sign of writing or
speaking.

Gemini is the willingness to try anything once, a need to wander and explore, the quick shifting of moods and attitudes being a basic characteristic that indicates a need for change. Versatility is the remarkable Gemini attribute. It is the capacity to investigate, perform, and relate over great areas for short periods of time and thus to connect all areas. It is mastery of design and perception, the power to conceptualize and create by putting elements together—people, colors, patterns. It is the reporter's mind, plus a brilliant ability to see things in objective, colorful arrangement. Strength lies in constant refreshment of outlook and joyful participation in all aspects of life.

Gemini is involvement with neighbors, family and relatives, telephones, arteries of news and communication—anything that enhances the human capacity for communication and self-expression. It is active, positive, and energetic, with an insatiable hunger for human interchange. Through Gemini bright and dark sides of personality merge and the mind has wings. As it flies it reflects the light of a boundless shining intellect. It is the development of varied talents from recognition of the duality of self.

Gemini is geared toward enjoying life to the fullest by finding, above all else, a means of expressing the inner self to the outside world.

CANCER
The Sign of the Crab

Cancer is the special relationship to home and involvement with the family unit. Maintaining harmony in the domestic sphere or improving conditions there is a major characteristic in this sector of the Zodiac. Cancer is attachment between two beings vibrating in sympathy with one another.

It is the comfort of a loving embrace, a tender generosity. Cancer is the place of shelter whenever there are lost or hungry souls in the night. Through Cancer we are fed, protected, comforted, and soothed. When the coldness of the world threatens, Cancer is there with gentle understanding. It is protection and understated loyalty, a medium of rich, living feeling that is both psychic and mystical. Highly intuitive, Cancer has knowledge that other signs do not possess. It is the wisdom of the soul.

It prefers the quiet contentment of the home and hearth to the busy search for earthly success and civilized pleasures. Still, there is a respect for worldly knowledge. Celebration of life comes through food. The sign is the muted light of warmth, security, and gladness, and its presence means nourishment. It rules fertility and the instinct to populate and raise young. It is growth of the soul. It is the ebb and flow of all our tides of feeling, involvements, habits, and customs.

Through Cancer is reflected the inner condition of all human beings, and therein lies the seed of knowledge out of which the soul will grow.

LEO
The Sign of the Lion

Leo is love. It represents the warmth, strength, and regeneration we feel through love. It is the radiance of life-giving light and the center of all attention and activity. It is passion, romance, adventure, and games. Pleasure, amusement, fun, and entertainment are all part of Leo. Based on the capacity for creative feeling and the desire to express love, Leo is the premier sign. It represents the unlimited outpouring of all that is warm and positive.

It is loyalty, dignity, responsibility, and command. Pride and nobility belong to Leo, and the dashing image of the knight in shining armor, of the hero, is part of Leo. It is a sense of high honor and kingly generosity born out of deep, noble love. It is the excitement of the sportsman, with all the unbeatable flair and style of success. It is a strong, unyielding will and true sense of personal justice, a respect for human freedom, and an enlightened awareness of people's needs.

Leo is involvement in the Self's awareness of personal talents and the desire and need to express them. At best it is forthrightness, courage and efficiency, authority and dignity, showmanship, and a talent for organization. Dependable and ardent, the Lion is characterized by individuality, positivism, and integrity.

It is the embodiment of human maturity, the effective individual in society, a virile creative force able to take chances and win. It is the love of laughter and the joy of making others happy. Decisive and enthusiastic, the Lion is the creative producer of the Zodiac It is the potential to light the way for others.

VIRGO
The Sign of the Virgin

Virgo is the sign of work and service. It is the symbol of the farmer at harvest time, and represents tireless efforts for the benefit of humanity, the joy of bringing the fruits of the Earth to the table of mankind. Celebration through work is the characteristic of this sign.

Sincerity, zeal, discipline, and devotion mark the sign of the Virgin.

The key word is purity, and in Virgo lies a potential for unlimited self-mastery. Virgo is the embodiment of perfected skill and refined talent. The thread of work is woven into the entire life of Virgo. All creativity is poured into streamlining a job, classifying a system, eradicating unnecessary elements of pure analysis. The true Virgo genius is found in separating the wheat from the chaff.

Spartan simplicity characterizes this sign, and Virgo battles the war between order and disorder. The need to arrange, assimilate, and categorize is great; it is the symbol of the diagnostician, the nurse, and the healer. Criticism and analysis describe this sign—pure, incisive wisdom and a shy appreciation of life's joys. All is devoted to the attainment of perfection and the ideal of self-mastery.

Virgo is the sign of health and represents the physical body as a functioning symbol of the mental and spiritual planes. It is the state of healing the ills of the human being with natural, temperate living. It is maturation of the ego as it passes from a self-centered phase to its awareness and devotion to humanity.

It is humanitarian, pragmatic, and scientific, with boundless curiosity. Focus and clarity of mind are the strong points, while strength of purpose and shy reserve underlie the whole sign. There is separateness, aloofness, and solitude for this beacon of the Zodiac. As a lighthouse guides ships, so Virgo shines.

LIBRA
The Sign of the Scales

Libra is the sign of human relationship, marriage, equality, and justice. It symbolizes the need of one human being for another, the capacity to find light, warmth, and life-giving love in relationship to another human being. It is union on any level—mental, sexual, emotional, or business. It is self-extension in a desire to find a partner with whom to share our joys. It is the capacity to recognize the needs of others and to develop to the fullest our powers of diplomacy, good taste, and refinement.

Libra is harmony, grace, aesthetic sensibility, and the personification of the spirit of companionship. It represents the skill to maintain balances and the ability to share mutually all life's benefits, trials, crises, and blessings. Libra is mastery at anticipation of another's needs or reactions. It is the exercise of simple justice with impartial delicacy.

It is the need to relate, to find a major person, place, or thing to sustain us and draw out our attention. It is growth through becoming awakened to the outside world and other people. It is the union of two loving souls in honesty, equality, mutual cooperation, and mutual accord.

SCORPIO
The Sign of the Scorpion

Scorpio is the sign of dark intensity, swirling passion, and sexual magnetism. It is the thirst for survival and regeneration that are the bases of sexual orientation and the creative impulses for self-expression. No other sign has such a profound instinct for survival and reproduction. Out of the abyss of emotions come a thousand creations, each one possessing a life of its own.

Scorpio is completion, determination, and endurance, fortified with enough stamina to outlive any enemy. It is the pursuit of goals despite any threat, warning, or obstacle that might stand in the way. It simply cannot be stopped. It knows when to wait and when to proceed. It is the constant state of readiness, a vibrant living force that constantly pumps out its rhythm from the depths of being.

Secretive and intimate, Scorpio symbolizes the self-directed creature with a will of steel. It is the flaming desire to create, manipulate, and control with a magician's touch. But the most mysterious quality is the capacity for metamorphosis, or total transformation.

This represents supremacy in the battle with dark unseen forces. It is the state of being totally fearless—the embodiment of truth and courage. It symbolizes the human capacity to face all danger and emerge supreme, to heal oneself. As a caterpillar spins its way into the darkness of a cocoon, Scorpio faces the end of existence, says goodbye to an old way of life, and goes through a kind of death—or total change.

Then, amid the dread of uncertainty, something remarkable happens. From hopelessness or personal crisis a new individual emerges, like a magnificent butterfly leaving behind its cocoon. It is a human being completely transformed and victorious. This is Scorpio.

SAGITTARIUS
The Sign of the Archer

Sagittarius is the sign of adventure and a thousand and one new experiences. It is the cause and purpose of every new attempt at adventure or self-understanding. It is the embodiment of enthusiasm, search for truth, and love of wisdom. Hope and optimism characterize this section of the Zodiac, and it is the ability to leave the past behind and set out again with positive resilience and a happy, cheerful outlook.

It is intelligence and exuberance, youthful idealism, and the desire to expand all horizons. It is the constant hatching of dreams, the hunger for knowledge, travel and experience. The goal is exploration itself.

Sagittarius is generosity, humor, and goodness of nature, backed up by the momentum of great expectations. It symbolizes the ability of people to be back in the race after having the most serious spills over the biggest hurdles. It is a healthy, positive outlook and the capacity to meet each new moment with unaffected buoyancy.

At this point in the Zodiac, greater conscious understanding begins to develop self-awareness and self-acceptance. It is an Olympian capacity to look upon the bright side and to evolve that aspect of mind we call conscience.

CAPRICORN
The Sign of the Sea Goat

Capricorn is the sign of structure and physical law. It rules depth, focus, and concentration. It is the symbol of success through perseverance, happiness through profundity. It is victory over disruption, and finds reality in codes set up by society and culture. It is the perpetuation of useful, tested patterns and a desire to protect what has already been established.

It is cautious, conservative, conscious of the passage of time, yet ageless. The Goat symbolizes the incorporation of reason into living and depth into loving.

Stability, responsibility, and fruitfulness through loyalty color this sector of the Zodiac with an undeniable and irrepressible awareness of success, reputation, and honor. Capricorn is the culmination of our earthly dreams, the pinnacle of our worldly life.

It is introspection and enlightenment through serious contemplation of the Self and its position in the world. It is mastery of understanding and the realization of dreams.

Capricorn is a winter blossom, a born professional with an aim of harmony and justice, beauty, grace, and success. It is the well-constructed pyramid: perfect and beautiful, architecturally correct, mysteriously implacable, and hard to know. It is highly organized and built on precise foundations to last and last and last. It is practical, useful yet magnificent and dignified, signifying permanence and careful planning. Like a pyramid, Capricorn has thick impenetrable walls, complex passageways, and false corridors. Yet somewhere at the heart of this ordered structure is the spirit of a mighty ruler.

AQUARIUS
The Sign of the Water Bearer

Aquarius is the symbol of idealized free society. It is the herding instinct in man as a social animal. It is the collection of heterogeneous elements of human consciousness in coherent peaceful coexistence. Friendship, goodwill, and harmonious contact are Aquarius attributes. It is founded on the principle of individual freedom and the brotherly love and respect for the rights of all men and women on Earth.

It is strength of will and purpose, altruism, and love of human fellowship. It is the belief in spontaneity and free choice, in the openness to live in a spirit of harmony and cooperation—liberated from restriction, repression, and conventional codes of conduct. It is the brilliant capacity to assimilate information instantaneously at the last minute and translate that information into immediate creative action, and so the result is to live in unpredictability.

This is the progressive mind, the collective mind—groups of people getting together to celebrate life. Aquarius is the child of the future, the utopian working for the betterment of the human race. Funds, charities, seeking better cities and better living conditions for others, involvement in great forms of media or communication, science or research in the hope of joining mankind to his higher self—this is all Aquarius.

It is invention, genius, revolution, discovery—instantaneous breakthrough from limitations. It's a departure from convention, eccentricity, the unexpected development that changes the course of history. It is the discovery of people and all the arteries that join them together. Aquarius is adventure, curiosity, exotic and alien appeal. It pours the water of life and intelligence for all humanity to drink. It is humanism, community, and the element of surprise.

PISCES
The Sign of the Fishes

Pisces is faith—undistracted, patient, all-forgiving faith—and therein lies the Pisces capacity for discipline, endurance, and stamina.

It is imagination and other-worldliness, the condition

of living a foggy, uncertain realm of poetry, music, and fantasy. Passive and compassionate, this sector of the Zodiac symbolizes the belief in the inevitability of life. It represents the view of life that everything exists in waves, like the sea. All reality as we know it is a dream, a magic illusion that must ultimately be washed away. Tides pull this way and that, whirlpools and undercurrents sweep across the bottom of life's existence, but in Pisces there is total acceptance of all tides, all rhythms, all possibilities. It is the final resolution of all personal contradictions and all confusing paradoxes.

It is the search for truth and honesty, and the devotion to love, utterly and unquestionably. It is the desire to act with wisdom, kindness, and responsibility and to welcome humanity completely free from scorn, malice, discrimination, or prejudice. It is total, all-embracing, idealistic love. It is the acceptance of two sides of a question at once and love through sacrifice.

Pisces is beyond reality. We are here today, but may be gone tomorrow. Let the tide of circumstances carry you where it will, for nothing is forever. As all things come, so must they go. In the final reel, all things must pass away. It is deliverance from sorrow through surrender to the infinite. The emotions are as vast as the ocean, yet in the pain of confusion there is hope in the secret cell of one's own heart. Pisces symbolizes liberation from pain through love, faith, and forgiveness.

THE SIGNS AND
THEIR KEY WORDS

		Positive	Negative
ARIES	self	courage, initiative, pioneer instinct	brash rudeness, selfish impetuosity
TAURUS	money	endurance, loyalty, wealth	obstinacy, gluttony
GEMINI	mind	versatility, communication	capriciousness, unreliability
CANCER	family	sympathy, homing instinct	clannishness, childishness
LEO	children	love, authority, integrity	egotism, force
VIRGO	work	purity, industry, analysis	faultfinding, cynicism
LIBRA	marriage	harmony, justice	vacillation, superficiality
SCORPIO	sex	survival, regeneration	vengeance, discord
SAGITTARIUS	travel	optimism, higher learning	lawlessness, irresponsibility
CAPRICORN	career	depth, responsibility	narrowness, gloom
AQUARIUS	friends	humanity, genius	perverse unpredictability
PISCES	faith	spiritual love, universality	diffusion, escapism

THE ELEMENTS AND
THE QUALITIES OF THE SIGNS

Every sign has both an element and a quality associated with it. The element indicates the basic makeup of the sign, and the quality describes the kind of activity associated with each.

Element	Sign	Quality	Sign
Fire	Aries Leo Sagittarius	Cardinal	Aries Libra Cancer Capricorn
Earth	Taurus Virgo Capricorn	Fixed	Taurus Leo Scorpio Aquarius
Air	Gemini Libra Aquarius	Mutable	Gemini Virgo Sagittarius Pisces
Water	Cancer Scorpio Pisces		

Signs can be grouped together according to their element and quality. Signs of the same element share many basic traits in common. They tend to form stable configurations and ultimately harmonious relationships. Signs of the same quality are often less harmonious, but share many dynamic potentials for growth and profound fulfillment.

The following pages describe these sign groupings in more detail.

The Fire Signs

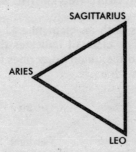

This is the fire group. On the whole these are emotional, volatile types, quick to anger, quick to forgive. They are adventurous, powerful people and act as a source of inspiration for everyone. They spark into action with immediate exuberant impulses. They are intelligent, self-involved, creative, and idealistic. They all share a certain vibrancy and glow that outwardly reflects an inner flame and passion for living.

The Earth Signs

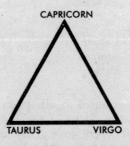

This is the earth group. They are in constant touch with the material world and tend to be conservative. Although they are all capable of spartan self-discipline, they are earthy, sensual people who are stimulated by the tangible, elegant, and luxurious. The thread of their lives is always practical, but they do fantasize and are often attracted to dark, mysterious, emotional people. They are like great cliffs overhanging the sea, forever married to the ocean but always resisting erosion from the dark, emotional forces that thunder at their feet.

The Air Signs

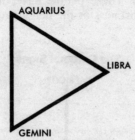

This is the air group. They are light, mental creatures desirous of contact, communication, and relationship. They are involved with people and the forming of ties on many levels. Original thinkers, they are the bearers of human news. Their language is their sense of word, color, style, and beauty. They provide an atmosphere suitable and pleasant for living. They add change and versatility to the scene, and it is through them that we can explore human intelligence and experience.

The Water Signs

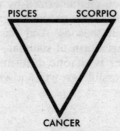

This is the water group. Through the water people, we are all joined together on emotional, nonverbal levels.

The water signs are silent, mysterious types whose magic hypnotizes even the most determined realist. They have uncanny perceptions about people and are as rich as the oceans when it comes to feeling, emotion, or imagination. They are sensitive, mystical creatures with memories that go back beyond time. Through water, life is sustained. These people have the potential for the depths of darkness or the heights of mysticism and art.

The Cardinal Signs

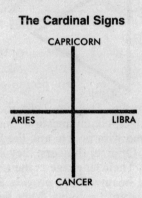

The cardinal signs present a picture of dynamism, activity, tremendous stress, and remarkable achievement. These people know the meaning of great change since their lives are often characterized by significant crises and major successes. The cardinal signs mark the beginning of the four seasons. And this combination is like a simultaneous storm of summer, fall, winter, and spring. The danger is chaotic diffusion of energy; the potential is irrepressible growth and victory.

The Fixed Signs

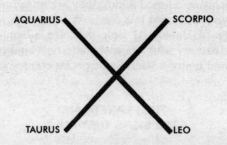

AQUARIUS   SCORPIO

TAURUS   LEO

Fixed signs are always establishing themselves in a given place or area of experience. Like explorers who arrive and plant a flag, these people claim a position from which they do not enjoy being deposed. They are staunch, stalwart, upright, trusty, honorable people, although their obstinacy is well-known. Their contribution is fixity, and they are the angels who support our visible world.

The Mutable Signs

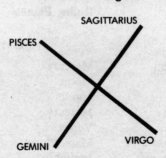

SAGITTARIUS

PISCES

GEMINI   VIRGO

Mutable people are versatile, sensitive, intelligent, nervous, and deeply curious about life. They are the translators of all energy. They often carry out or complete tasks initiated by others. People from mutable signs have highly developed minds; they are imaginative and jumpy and think and talk a lot. At worst their lives are a Tower of Babel. At best they are adaptable and ready creatures who can assimilate one kind of experience and enjoy it while anticipating coming changes.

THE PLANETS AND
THE SIGNS THEY RULE

The signs of the Zodiac are linked to the planets in the following way. Each sign is governed or ruled by one or more planets. No matter where the planets are located in the sky at any given moment, they still rule their respective signs. When they travel through the signs they rule, they have special dignity and their effects are stronger.

Following is a list of the planets and the signs they rule. After you read the definitions of the planets from pages 88 to 96, see if you can determine how the planet ruling *your* Sun sign has affected your life.

Signs	Ruling Planets
Aries	Mars, Pluto
Taurus	Venus
Gemini	Mercury
Cancer	Moon
Leo	Sun
Virgo	Mercury
Libra	Venus
Scorpio	Mars, Pluto
Sagittarius	Jupiter
Capricorn	Saturn
Aquarius	Saturn, Uranus
Pisces	Jupiter, Neptune

THE ZODIAC AND
THE HUMAN BODY

The signs of the Zodiac are linked to the human body in a direct relationship. Each sign has a part of the body with which it is associated.

It is traditionally believed that surgery is best performed when the Moon is passing through a sign *other* than the sign associated with the part of the body upon which an operation is to be performed. But often the presence of the Moon in a particular sign will bring the focus of attention to that very part of the body under medical scrutiny.

The principles of medical astrology are complex and beyond the scope of this introduction. We can, however, list the signs of the Zodiac and the parts of the human body connected with them. Once you learn these correspondences, you'll be amazed at how accurate they are.

Signs	Human Body
Aries	Head, brain, face, upper jaw
Taurus	Throat, neck, lower jaw
Gemini	Hands, arms, lungs, nerves
Cancer	Stomach, breasts, womb, liver
Leo	Heart, spine
Virgo	Intestines, liver
Libra	Kidneys, lower back
Scorpio	Sex and eliminative organs
Sagittarius	Hips, thighs, liver
Capricorn	Skin, bones, teeth, knees
Aquarius	Circulatory system, lower legs
Pisces	Feet, tone of being

THE ZODIACAL HOUSES
AND THE RISING SIGN

Apart from the month and day of birth, the exact time of birth is another vital factor in the determination of an accurate horoscope. Not only do planets move with great speed, but one must know how far the Earth has turned during the day. That way you can determine exactly where the planets are located with respect to the precise birthplace of an individual. This makes your horoscope *your* horoscope.

The horoscope sets up a kind of framework around which the life of an individual grows like wild ivy, this way and that, weaving its way around the trellis of the natal positions of the planets. The year of birth tells us the positions of the distant, slow-moving planets Jupiter, Saturn, Uranus, Neptune, and Pluto. The month of birth indicates the Sun sign, or birth sign as it is commonly called, as well as indicating the positions of the rapidly moving planets Venus, Mercury, and Mars. The day of birth, as well as the time, locates the position of our Moon. And the moment of birth—the exact hour and minute—determines the houses through what is called the Ascendant, or Rising sign.

The illustration on the next page shows the flat chart, or natural wheel, an astrologer uses. The inner circle of the wheel is labeled 1 through 12. These 12 divisions are known as the houses of the Zodiac.

The 1st house always starts from the position marked E, which corresponds to the eastern horizon. The rest of the houses 2 through 12 follow around in a "counterclockwise" direction. The point where each house starts is known as a cusp, or edge.

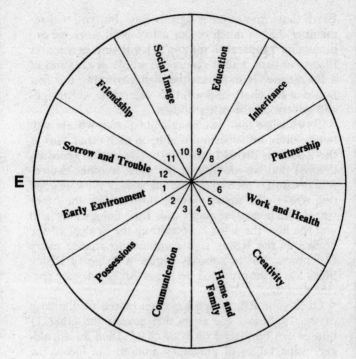

The 12 Houses of the Zodiac

The cusp, or edge, of the 1st house (point E) is where an astrologer would place your Rising sign, the Ascendant. The Rising sign is very important in a horoscope, as it defines your self-image, outlook, physical constitution, early environment, and whole orientation to life. And, as already mentioned, the exact time of your birth determines your Rising sign. Let's see how this works.

As the Earth rotates on its axis once every 24 hours, each one of the 12 signs of the Zodiac appears to be "rising" on the horizon, with a new one appearing about every two hours. Actually it is the turning of the

Earth that exposes each sign to view, but you will remember that in much of our astrological work we are
discussing "apparent" motion. This Rising sign marks
the Ascendant, and it colors the whole orientation of
a horoscope. It indicates the sign governing the first
house of the chart, and will thus determine which signs
will govern all the other houses.

To visualize this idea, imagine two color wheels with
twelve divisions superimposed upon each other. Just as
the Zodiac is divided into twelve star groups (constel-
lations) that we identify as the signs, another twelvefold division is used to denote the houses. Now imagine
one wheel (the signs) moving slowly while the other
wheel (the houses) remains still. This analogy may help
you see how the signs keep shifting the "color" of the
houses as the Rising sign continues to change every
two hours. But to simplify things, a Table of Rising
Signs has been provided on pages 20–21 for your specific Sun sign.

Once your Rising sign has been placed on the cusp
of the 1st house, the signs that govern the other 11
houses can be placed on your chart. Then an astrologer, using tables of planetary motion, can locate the
positions of all the planets in their appropriate houses.
The house where your Sun sign is describes your basic
character and your fundamental drives. And the houses
where the other planets are in your chart suggest the
areas of life on Earth in which you will be most likely
to focus your constant energy and center your activity.

The illustration on page 83 briefly identifies each of
the 12 houses of the Zodiac. Now the pages that follow
provide a detailed discussion of the meanings of the
houses. In the section after the houses we will define
all the known planets of the solar system, with a separate section on the Moon, in order to acquaint you
with more of the astrological vocabulary you will be
meeting again and again.

THE MEANING OF THE HOUSES

The twelve houses of every horoscope represent areas of life on Earth, or regions of worldly experience. Depending on which sign of the Zodiac was rising on the eastern horizon at the moment of birth, the activity of each house will be "colored" by the zodiacal sign on its cusp, or edge. In other words, the sign falling on the first house will determine what signs will fall on the rest of the houses.

1 The first house determines the basic orientation to all of life on Earth. It indicates the body type, face, head, and brain. It rules your self-image, or the way others see you because of the way you see your self. This is the Ascendant of the horoscope and is the focus of energies of your whole chart. It acts like a prism through which all of the planetary light passes and is reflected in your life. It colors your outlook and influences everything you do and see.

2 This is the house of finances. Here is your approach to money and materialism in general. It indicates where the best sources are for you to improve your financial condition and your earning power as a whole. It indicates chances for gain or loss. It describes your values, alliances, and assets.

3 This is the house of the day-to-day mind. Short trips, communication, and transportation are associated with this house. It deals with routines, brothers and sisters, relatives, neighbors, and the near environment at hand. Language, letters, and the tools for transmitting information are included in third-house matters.

4 This is the house that describes your home and home life, parents, and childhood in the sense of indicating the kind of roots you come from. It symbolizes your present home and domestic situation and reflects your need for privacy and retreat from the world, indicating, of course, what kind of scene you require.

5 Pleasure, love affairs, amusements, parties, creativity, children. This is the house of passion and courtship and of expressing your talents, whatever they are. It is related to the development of your personal life and the capacity to express feeling and enjoy romance.

6 This is the house of work. Here there are tasks to be accomplished and maladjustments to be corrected. It is the house of health as well, and describes some of the likely places where physical health difficulties may appear. It rules routines, regimen, necessary jobs as opposed to a chosen career, army, navy, police—people employed, co-workers, and those in service to others. It indicates the individual's ability to harvest the fruit of his own efforts.

7 This is the house of marriage, partnership, and unions. It represents the alter ego, all people other than yourself, open confrontation with the public. It describes your partner and the condition of partnership as you discern it. In short, it is your "take" on the world. It indicates your capacity to make the transition from courtship to marriage and specifically what you seek out in others.

8 This is the house of deep personal transition, sex as a form of mutual surrender and interchange between human beings. It is the release from tensions and the completion of the creative processes. The eighth house also has to do with taxes, inheritances, and the finances of others, as well as death as the ending of cycles and crises.

9 This is the house of the higher mind, philosophy, religion, and the expression of personal conscience through moral codes. It indicates political leanings, ethical views, and the capacity of the individual for a broader perspective and deeper understanding of himself in relation to society. It is through the ninth house that you make great strides in learning and travel to distant places and come to know yourself through study, dreams, and wide experience.

10 This is the house of career, honor, and prestige. It marks the culmination of worldly experience and indicates the highest point you can reach, what you look up to, and how high you can go in this lifetime. It describes your parents, employers, and how you view authority figures, the condition and direction of your profession, and your position in the community.

11 This is the house of friendships. It describes your social behavior, your views on humanity, and your hopes, aspirations, and wishes for an ideal life. It will indicate what kinds of groups, clubs, organizations, and friendships you tend to form and what you seek out in your chosen alliances other than with your mate or siblings. This house suggests the capacity for the freedom and unconventionality that an individual is seeking, his sense of his connection with mankind, and the definition of his goals, personal and social.

12 This is the house of seclusion, secret wisdom, and self-incarceration. It indicates our secret enemies as well, in the sense that there may be persons, feelings, or memories we are trying to escape. It is self-undoing in that this house acts against the ego in order to find a higher, more universal purpose. It rules prisons, hospitals, charities, and selfless service. It is the house of unfinished psychic business.

THE PLANETS OF THE SOLAR SYSTEM

The planets of the solar system all travel around the Sun at different speeds and different distances. Taken with the Sun, they all distribute individual intelligence and ability throughout the entire chart.

The planets modify the influence of the Sun in a chart according to their own particular natures, strengths, and positions. Their positions must be calculated for each year and day, and their function and expression in a horoscope will change as they move from one area of the Zodiac to another.

Following, you will find brief statements of their pure meanings.

THE SUN

The Sun is the center of existence. Around this flaming sphere all the planets revolve in endless orbits. Our star is constantly sending out its beams of light and energy without which no life on Earth would be possible. In astrology it symbolizes everything we are trying to become, the center around which all of our activity in life will always revolve. It is the symbol of our basic nature and describes the natural and constant thread that runs through everything that we do from birth to death on this planet.

Everything in the horoscope ultimately revolves around this singular body. Although other forces may be prominent in the charts of some individuals, still the

THE SUN

Sun is the total nucleus of being and symbolizes the complete potential of every human being alive. It is vitality and the life force. Your whole essence comes from the position of the Sun.

You are always trying to express the Sun according to its position by house and sign. Possibility for all development is found in the Sun, and it marks the fundamental character of your personal radiations all around you.

It symbolizes strength, vigor, ardor, generosity, and the ability to function effectively as a mature individual and a creative force in society. It is consciousness of the gift of life. The undeveloped solar nature is arrogant pushy, undependable, and proud, and is constantly using force.

MERCURY

Mercury is the planet closest to the Sun. It races around our star, gathering information and translating it to the rest of the system. Mercury represents your capacity to understand the desires of your own will and to translate those desires into action.

MERCURY

In other words it is the planet of mind and the power of communication. Through Mercury we develop an ability to think, write, speak, and observe—to become aware of the world around us. It colors our attitudes and vision of the world, as well as our capacity to communicate our inner responses to the outside world. Some people who have serious disabilities in their power of verbal communication have often wrongly been described as people lacking intelligence.

Although this planet (and its position in the horoscope) indicates your power to communicate your thoughts and perceptions to the world, intelligence is something deeper. Intelligence is distributed throughout all the planets. It is the relationship of the planets to each other that truly describes what we call intelligence. Mercury rules speaking, language, mathematics, draft and design, students, messengers, young people, offices, teachers, and any pursuits where the mind of man has wings.

VENUS

Venus is beauty. It symbolizes the harmony and radiance of a rare and elusive quality: beauty itself. It is refinement and delicacy, softness and charm. In astrology it indicates grace, balance, and the aesthetic sense. Where Venus is we see beauty, a gentle drawing in of energy and the need for satisfaction and completion. It is a special touch that finishes off rough edges.

VENUS

Venus is the planet of sensitivity and affection, and it is always the place for that other elusive phenomenon: love. Venus describes our sense of what is beautiful and loving. Poorly developed, it is vulgar, tasteless, and self-indulgent. But its ideal is the flame of spiritual love—Aphrodite, goddess of love, and the sweetness and power of personal beauty.

MARS

Mars is raw, crude energy. The planet next to Earth but outward from the Sun is a fiery red sphere that charges through the horoscope with force and fury. It represents the way you reach out for new adventure and new experience. It is energy drive, initiative, courage, daring. It is the power to start something and see it through. It can be thoughtless, cruel and wild, angry and hostile, causing cuts, burns, scalds, wounds. It can stab its way through a chart, or it can be the symbol of healthy spirited adventure, well-channeled constructive power to begin and keep up the drive.

MARS

If you have trouble starting things, if you lack the get-up-and-go to start the ball rolling, if you lack aggressiveness and self-confidence, chances are there's another planet influencing your Mars. Mars rules soldiers, butchers, surgeons, salespeople—in general any field that requires daring, bold skill, operational technique, or self-promotion.

JUPITER

Jupiter is the largest planet of the solar system. Planet Jupiter rules good luck and good cheer, health, wealth, optimism, happiness, success, joy. It is the symbol of opportunity and always opens the way for new possibilities in your life. It rules exuberance, enthusiasm, wisdom, knowledge, generosity, and all forms of expansion in general. It rules actors, statesmen, clerics, professional people, religion, publishing, and the distribution of many people over large areas.

JUPITER

Sometimes Jupiter makes you think you deserve everything, and you become sloppy, wasteful, careless and rude, prodigal and lawless, in the illusion that nothing can ever go wrong. Then there is the danger of your showing overconfidence, exaggeration, undependability, and overindulgence.

Jupiter is the minimization of limitation and the emphasis on spirituality and potential. It is the thirst for knowledge and higher learning.

SATURN

Saturn circles our system in dark splendor with its mysterious rings, forcing us to be awakened to whatever we have neglected in the past. It will present real puzzles and problems to be solved, causing delays, obstacles, and hindrances. By doing so, Saturn stirs our own sensitivity to those areas where we are laziest.

SATURN

Here we must patiently develop method, and only through painstaking effort can our ends be achieved. It brings order to a horoscope and imposes reason just where we are feeling least reasonable. By creating limitations and boundary, Saturn shows the consequences of being human and demands that we accept the changing cycles inevitable in human life. Saturn rules time, old age, and sobriety. It can bring depression, gloom, jealousy, and greed, or serious acceptance of responsibilities out of which success will develop. With Saturn there is nothing to do but face facts. It rules laborers, stones, granite, rocks, and crystals.

THE OUTER PLANETS: URANUS, NEPTUNE, PLUTO

Uranus, Neptune, and Pluto are the outer planets. They liberate human beings from cultural conditioning, and in that sense are the lawbreakers. In early times it was thought that Saturn was the last planet of the solar system—the outer limit beyond which we could never go. The discovery of the next three planets beyond Saturn ushered in new phases of human history, revolution, and technology.

URANUS

Uranus rules unexpected change, upheaval, revolution. It is the symbol of total independence and asserts the freedom of an individual from all restriction and restraint. It is a breakthrough planet and indicates talent, originality, and genius in a horoscope. It usually causes last-minute reversals and changes of plan, unwanted separations, accidents, catastrophes, and eccentric behavior. It can add irrational rebelliousness and perverse bohemianism to a personality or a streak of unaffected brilliance in science and art.

URANUS

Uranus rules technology, aviation, and all forms of electrical and electronic advancement. It governs great leaps forward and topsy-turvy situations, and always turns things around at the last minute. Its effects are difficult to predict, since it rules sudden last-minute decisions and events that come like lightning out of the blue.

NEPTUNE

Neptune dissolves existing reality the way the sea erodes the cliffs beside it. Its effects are subtle like the ringing of a buoy's bell in the fog. It suggests a reality higher than definition can usually describe. It awakens a sense of higher responsibility often causing guilt, worry, anxieties, or delusions. Neptune is associated with all forms of escape and can make things seem a certain way so convincingly that you are absolutely sure of something that eventually turns out to be quite different.

NEPTUNE

It is the planet of illusion and therefore governs the invisible realms that lie beyond our ordinary minds, beyond our simple factual ability to prove what is "real." Treachery, deceit, disillusionment, and disappointment are linked to Neptune. It describes a vague reality that promises eternity and the divine, yet in a manner so complex that we cannot really fathom it at all. At its worst Neptune is a cheap intoxicant; at its best it is the poetry, music, and inspiration of the higher planes of spiritual love. It has dominion over movies, photographs, and much of the arts.

PLUTO

Pluto lies at the outpost of our system and therefore rules finality in a horoscope—the final closing of chapters in your life, the passing of major milestones and points of development from which there is no return. It is a final wipeout, a closeout, an evacuation. It is a subtle but powerful catalyst in all transformations that occur. It creates, destroys, then recreates. Sometimes Pluto starts its influence with a minor event or insignificant incident that might even go unnoticed. Slowly but surely, little by little, everything changes, until at last there has been a total transformation in the area of your life where Pluto has been operating. It rules mass thinking and the trends that society first rejects, then adopts, and finally outgrows.

PLUTO

Pluto rules the dead and the underworld—all the powerful forces of creation and destruction that go on all the time beneath, around, and above us. It can bring a lust for power with strong obsessions.

It is the planet that rules the metamorphosis of the caterpillar into a butterfly, for it symbolizes the capacity to change totally and forever a person's lifestyle, way of thought, and behavior.

THE MOON

Exactly how does the Moon affect us psychologically and psychically? We know it controls the tides. We understand how it affects blood rhythm and body tides, together with all the chemical fluids that constitute our physical selves. Astronauts have walked upon its surface, and our scientists are now studying and analyzing data that will help determine the age of our satellite, its origin, and makeup.

THE MOON

But the true mystery of that small body as it circles our Earth each month remains hidden. Is it really a dead, lifeless body that has no light or heat of its own, reflecting only what the gigantic Sun throws toward it? Is it a sensitive reflecting device, which translates the blinding, billowing energy from our star into a language our bodies can understand?

In astrology, the Moon is said to rule our feelings, customs, habits, and moods. As the Sun is the constant, ever shining source of life in daytime, the Moon is our nighttime mother, lighting up the night and swiftly moving, reflecting ever so rapidly the changing phases of behavior and personality. If we feel happy or joyous, or we notice certain habits and repetitive feelings that bubble up from our dark centers then vanish as quickly as they appeared, very often it is the position of the Moon that describes these changes.

THE MOON IN ALL SIGNS

The Moon moves quickly through the Zodiac, that is, through all twelve signs of our Sun's apparent path. It stays in each sign for about 2¼ days. During its brief stay in a given sign, the moods and responses of people are always colored by the nature of that sign, any planets located there at that time, or any other heavenly bodies placed in such a way that the Moon will pick up their "vibration" as well. It's astonishing to observe how clearly the Moon changes people's interests and involvements as it moves along.

The following section gives brief descriptions of the Moon's influence in each sign.

MOON IN ARIES

There's excitement in the air. Some new little thing appears, and people are quick and full of energy and enterprise, ready for something new and turning on to a new experience. There's not much patience or hesitation, doubt or preoccupation with guilty self-damning recriminations. What's needed is action. People feel like putting their plans into operation. Pleasure and adventure characterize the mood, and it's time for things to change, pick up, improve. Confidence, optimism, positive feeling pervade the air. Sick people take a turn for the better. Life stirs with a feeling of renewal. People react bravely to challenges, with a sense of courage and dynamism. Self-reliance is the key word, and people minimize their problems and maximize the power to exercise freedom of the will. There is an air of abruptness and shortness of consideration, as people are feeling the courage of their convictions to do something for themselves. Feelings are strong and intuitive, and the mood is idealistic and freedom-oriented.

MOON IN TAURUS

Here the mood is just as pleasure loving, but less idealistic. Now the concerns are more materialistic, money-oriented, down-to-earth. The mood is stable, diligent, thoughtful, deliberate. It is a time when feelings are rich and deep, with a profound appreciation of the good things the world has to offer and the pleasures of the sensations. It is a period when people's minds are serious, realistic, and devoted to the increases and improvements of property and possessions and acquisition of wealth. There is a conservative tone, and people are fixed in their views, needing to add to their stability in every way. Assessment of assets, criticism, and the execution of tasks are strong involvements of the Taurus Moon when financial matters demand attention. It is devotion to security on a financial and emotional level. It is a fertile time, when ideas can begin to take root and grow.

MOON IN GEMINI

There is a rapid increase in movement. People are going places, exchanging ideas and information. Gossip and news travel fast under a Gemini Moon, because people are naturally involved with communication, finding out things from some, passing on information to others. Feelings shift to a mental level now, and people feel and say things that are sincere at the moment but lack the root and depth to endure much beyond the moment. People are involved with short-term engagements, quick trips. There is a definite need for changing the scene. You'll find people flirtatious and talkative, experimental and easygoing, falling into encounters they hadn't planned on. The mind is quick and active, with powers of writing and speaking greatly enhanced. Radio, television, letters, newspapers, magazines are in the spotlight with the Moon in Gemini, and new chances pop up for self-expression, with new people involved. Relatives and neighbors are tuned in to you and you to them. Take advantage of this fluidity of mind. It can rescue you from worldly involvements and get you into new surroundings for a short while.

MOON IN CANCER

Now you'll see people heading home. People turn their attention inward to their place of residence under a Cancer Moon. The active, changeable moods of yesterday vanish, and people settle in as if they were searching for a nest of security. Actually people are retiring, seeking to find peace and quiet within themselves. That's what they're feeling when they prefer to stay home rather than go out with a crowd of people to strange places. They need the warmth and comfort of the family and hearth. Maybe they feel anxious and insecure from the hustle and bustle of the workaday world. Maybe they're just tired. But it's definitely a time of tender need for emotional sustenance. It's a time for nostalgia and returning to times and places that once nourished deeply. Thoughts of parents, family, and old associations come to people. The heritage of their family ties holds them strongly now. These are personal needs that must be fed. Moods are deep and mysterious and sometimes sad. People are silent, psychic, and imaginative during this period. It's a fruitful time when people respond to love, food, and all the comforts of the inner world.

MOON IN LEO

The shift is back out in the world, and people are born
again, like kids. They feel zestful, passionate, exuberant and need plenty of attention. They're interested in
having a good time, enjoying themselves, and the world
of entertainment takes over for a while. Places of
amusement, theaters, parties, sprees, a whole gala of
glamorous events, characterize this stage of the Moon's
travel. Gracious, lavish hosting and a general feeling of
buoyancy and flamboyance are in the air. It's a time of
sunny, youthful fun when people are in the mood to
take chances and win. The approach is direct, ardent,
and strong. Bossy, authoritarian feelings predominate,
and people throw themselves forward for all they're
worth. Flattery is rampant, but the ego is vibrant and
flourishing with the kiss of life, romance, and love.
Speculation is indicated, and it's usually a time to go
out and try your hand at love. Life is full and rich as
a summer meadow, and feelings are warm.

MOON IN VIRGO

The party's over. Eyelashes are on the table. This is a
time for cleaning up after the merrymakers have gone
home. People are now concerned with sobering up and
getting personal affairs straight, clearing up any con-
fusions or undefined feelings from the night before,
and generally attending to the practical business of
doctoring up after the party. People are back at work,
concerned with necessary, perhaps tedious tasks—paying bills, fixing and adjusting things, and generally pu-
rifying their lives, streamlining their affairs, and
involving themselves with work and service to the community. Purity is the key word in personal habits, diet,
and emotional needs. Propriety and coolness take the
place of yesterday's devil-may-care passion, and the results are a detached, inhibited period under a Virgo

Moon. Feelings are not omitted; they are merely subjected to the scrutiny of the mind and thus purified. Health comes to the fore, and people are interested in clearing up problems.

MOON IN LIBRA

Here there is a mood of harmony, when people strive to join with other people in a bond of peace and justice. At this time people need relationships and often seek the company of others in a smooth-flowing feeling of love, beauty, and togetherness. People make efforts to understand other people, and though it's not the best time to make decisions, many situations keep presenting themselves from the outside to change plans and offer new opportunities. There is a general search for accord between partners, and differences are explored as similarities are shared. The tone is concilatory, and the mood is one of cooperation, patience, and tolerance. People do not generally feel independent, and sometimes this need to share or lean on others disturbs them. It shouldn't. This is the moment for uniting and sharing, for feeling a mutual flow of kindness and tenderness between people. The air is ingratiating and sometimes lacks stamina, courage, and a consistent, definite point of view. But it is a time favoring the condition of beauty and the development of all forms of art.

MOON IN SCORPIO

This is not a mood of sharing. It's driving, intense, brooding—full of passion and desire. Its baser aspects are the impulses of selfishness, cruelty, and the pursuit of animal drives and appetites. There is a craving for excitement and a desire to battle and win in a bloodthirsty war for survival. It is competitive and ruthless, sarcastic and easily bruised, highly sexual and touchy, without being especially tender. Retaliation, jealousy, and revenge can be felt too during this time. Financial involvements, debts, and property issues arise now. Powerful underworld forces are at work here, and great care is needed to transform ignorance into wisdom, to keep the mind from descending into the lower depths. During the Moon's stay in Scorpio we contact the dark undercurrents swirling around and get in touch with a magical part of our natures. Interest lies in death, inheritance, and the powers of rebirth and regeneration.

MOON IN SAGITTARIUS

Here the mind climbs out of the depths, and people are involved with the higher, more enlightened, and conscious facets of their personality. There's a renewed interest in learning, education, and philosophy, and a new involvement with ethics, morals, national and international issues: a concern with looking for a better way to live. It's a time of general improvement, with people feeling more deeply hopeful and optimistic. They are dreaming of new places, new possibilities, new horizons. They are emerging from the abyss and leaving the past behind, with their eyes gazing toward the new horizon. They decide to travel, or renew their contacts with those far away. They question their religious beliefs and investigate new areas of metaphysical inquiry. It's a time for adventure, sports, playing the field—people have their eye on new possibilities. They are bored with depression and details. They feel restless and optimistic, joyous and delighted to be alive. Thoughts revolve around adventure, travel, liberation.

MOON IN CAPRICORN

When the Moon moves into Capricorn, things slow down considerably. People require a quiet, organized, and regularized condition. Their minds are sober and realistic, and they are methodically going about bringing their dreams and plans into reality. They are more conscious of what is standing between them and success, and during this time they take definite, decisive steps to remove any obstacles from their path. They are cautious, suspicious, sometimes depressed, discouraged, and gloomy, but they are more determined than ever to accomplish their tasks. They take care of responsibilities now, wake up to facts, and wrestle with problems and dilemmas of this world. They are politically minded and concerned with social convention now, and it is under a Capricorn Moon that conditioning and conformity elicit the greatest responses. People are moderate and serious and surround themselves with what is most familiar. They want predictable situations and need time to think deeply and deliberately about all issues. It's a time for planning.

MOON IN AQUARIUS

Spontaneity replaces the sober predictability of yesterday. Now events, people, and situations pop up, and you take advantage of unsought opportunities and can expect the unexpected. Surprises, reversals, and shifts in plans mark this period. There is a resurgence of optimism, and things you wouldn't expect to happen suddenly do. What you were absolutely sure was going to happen simply doesn't. Here there is a need for adventure born from a healthy curiosity that characterizes people's moods. Unrealistic utopias are dreamed of, and it is from such idealistic dreams that worlds of the future are built. There is a renewed interest in friendship, comradeship, community, and union on high planes of mental and spiritual companionship. People free each other from grudges or long-standing deadlocks, and there is a hopeful joining of hands in a spirit of love and peace. People don't feel like sticking to previous plans, and they must be able to respond to new situations at the last minute. People need freedom. Groups of people come together and meet, perhaps for a common purpose of having dinner or hearing music, and leave knowing each other better.

MOON IN PISCES

Flashes of brilliant insight and mysterious knowledge characterize the Moon's passage in Pisces. Sometimes valuable "truths" seem to emerge which, later in the light of day, turn out to be false. This is a time of poetry, intuition, and music, when worldly realities can be the most illusory and unreliable of all. There are often feelings of remorse, guilt, or sorrow connected with a Pisces Moon—sorrow from the childhood or family or past. Confusion, anxiety, worry, and a host of imagined pains and sorrows may drag you down until you cannot move or think. Often there are connections with hospitals, prisons, alcohol, drugs, and lower forms of escape. It is a highly emotional time, when the feelings and compassion for humanity and all people everywhere rise to the surface of your being. Mysteries of society and the soul now rise to demand solutions, but often the riddles posed during this period have many answers that all seem right. It is more a time for inner reflection than positive action. It is a time when poetry and music float to the surface of the being, and for the creative artist it is the richest source of inspiration.

MOON TABLES
CORRECTION FOR NEW YORK TIME, FIVE HOURS WEST OF GREENWICH

Atlanta, Boston, Detroit, Miami, Washington, Montreal, Ottawa, Quebec, Bogota, Havana, Lima, Santiago......................Same time

Chicago, New Orleans, Houston, Winnipeg, Churchill, Mexico City..............................Deduct 1 hour

Albuquerque, Denver, Phoenix, El Paso, Edmonton, Helena...................................Deduct 2 hours

Los Angeles, San Francisco, Reno, Portland, Seattle, Vancouver.......................Deduct 3 hours

Honolulu, Anchorage, Fairbanks, Kodiak...Deduct 5 hours

Nome, Samoa, Tonga, Midway.............Deduct 6 hours

Halifax, Bermuda, San Juan, Caracas, La Paz, Barbados ....Add 1 hour

St. John's, Brasilia, Rio de Janeiro, Sao Paulo, Buenos Aires, Montevideo...................Add 2 hours

Azores, Cape Verde Islands....................Add 3 hours

Canary Islands, Madeira, Reykjavik ....Add 4 hours

London, Paris, Amsterdam, Madrid, Lisbon, Gibraltar, Belfast, Rabat....................Add 5 hours

Frankfurt, Rome, Oslo, Stockholm, Prague, Belgrade......................................Add 6 hours

Bucharest, Beirut, Tel Aviv, Athens, Istanbul, Cairo, Alexandria, Cape Town, Johannesburg......Add 7 hours

Moscow, Leningrad, Baghdad, Dhahran, Addis Ababa, Nairobi, Teheran, Zanzibar...Add 8 hours

Bombay, Calcutta, Sri Lanka..............Add 10 ½ hours

Hong Kong, Shanghai, Manila, Peking, Perth ....Add 13 hours

Tokyo, Okinawa, Darwin, Pusan ....Add 14 hours

Sydney, Melbourne, Port Moresby, Guam ....Add 15 hours

Auckland, Wellington, Suva, Wake...........Add 17 hours

1999 MOON SIGN DATES—NEW YORK TIME

JANUARY			FEBRUARY			MARCH		
Day	Moon Enters		Day	Moon Enters		Day	Moon Enters	
1.	Cancer	3:16 am	1.	Virgo	8:38 pm	1.	Virgo	5:06 am
2.	Cancer		2.	Virgo		2.	Virgo	
3.	Leo	5:32 am	3.	Virgo		3.	Libra	1:35 pm
4.	Leo		4.	Libra	4:57 am	4.	Libra	
5.	Virgo	10:50 am	5.	Libra		5.	Libra	
6.	Virgo		6.	Scorp.	4:07 pm	6.	Scorp.	0:23 am
7.	Libra	7:54 pm	7.	Scorp.		7.	Scorp.	
8.	Libra		8.	Scorp.		8.	Sagitt.	0:47 pm
9.	Libra		9.	Sagitt.	4:39 am	9.	Sagitt.	
10.	Scorp.	7:50 am	10.	Sagitt.		10.	Sagitt.	
11.	Scorp.		11.	Capric.	4:11 pm	11.	Capric.	0:55 am
12.	Sagitt.	8:24 pm	12.	Capric.		12.	Capric.	
13.	Sagitt.		13.	Capric.		13.	Aquar.	10:33 am
14.	Sagitt.		14.	Aquar.	0:58 am	14.	Aquar.	
15.	Capric.	7:30 am	15.	Aquar.		15.	Pisces	4:31 pm
16.	Capric.		16.	Pisces	6:41 am	16.	Pisces	
17.	Aquar.	4:12 pm	17.	Pisces		17.	Aries	7:14 pm
18.	Aquar.		18.	Aries	10:07 am	18.	Aries	
19.	Pisces	10:41 pm	19.	Aries		19.	Taurus	8:10 pm
20.	Pisces		20.	Taurus	0:30 pm	20.	Taurus	
21.	Pisces		21.	Taurus		21.	Gemini	9:06 pm
22.	Aries	3:26 am	22.	Gemini	2:55 pm	22.	Gemini	
23.	Aries		23.	Gemini		23.	Cancer	11:34 pm
24.	Taurus	6:53 am	24.	Cancer	6:10 pm	24.	Cancer	
25.	Taurus		25.	Cancer		25.	Cancer	
26.	Gemini	9:30 am	26.	Leo	10:45 pm	26.	Leo	4:23 am
27.	Gemini		27.	Leo		27.	Leo	
28.	Cancer	11:58 am	28.	Leo		28.	Virgo	11:35 am
29.	Cancer					29.	Virgo	
30.	Leo	3:17 pm				30.	Libra	8:50 pm
31.	Leo					31.	Libra	

Summer time to be considered where applicable.

1999 MOON SIGN DATES—NEW YORK TIME

APRIL		MAY		JUNE	
Day Moon Enters		**Day Moon Enters**		**Day Moon Enters**	
1. Libra		1. Scorp.		1. Capric.	
2. Scorp.	7:50 am	2. Sagitt.	2:37 am	2. Capric.	
3. Scorp.		3. Sagitt.		3. Aquar.	8:38 am
4. Sagitt.	8:08 pm	4. Capric.	3:13 am	4. Aquar.	
5. Sagitt.		5. Capric.		5. Pisces	6:02 pm
6. Sagitt.		6. Capric.		6. Pisces	
7. Capric.	8:40 am	7. Aquar.	2:41 am	7. Pisces	
8. Capric.		8. Aquar.		8. Aries	0:09 am
9. Aquar.	7:25 pm	9. Pisces	11:17 am	9. Aries	
10. Aquar.		10. Pisces		10. Taurus	2:44 am
11. Aquar.		11. Aries	3:54 pm	11. Taurus	
12. Pisces	2:36 am	12. Aries		12. Gemini	2:49 am
13. Pisces		13. Taurus	4:57 pm	13. Gemini	
14. Aries	5:47 am	14. Taurus		14. Cancer	2:15 am
15. Aries		15. Gemini	4:08 pm	15. Cancer	
16. Taurus	6:08 am	16. Gemini		16. Leo	3:08 am
17. Taurus		17. Cancer	3:40 pm	17. Leo	
18. Gemini	5:40 am	18. Cancer		18. Virgo	7:13 am
19. Gemini		19. Leo	5:38 pm	19. Virgo	
20. Cancer	6:28 am	20. Leo		20. Libra	3:11 pm
21. Cancer		21. Virgo	11:16 pm	21. Libra	
22. Leo	10:07 am	22. Virgo		22. Libra	
23. Leo		23. Virgo		23. Scorp.	2:19 am
24. Virgo	5:05 pm	24. Libra	8:30 am	24. Scorp.	
25. Virgo		25. Libra		25. Sagitt.	2:52 pm
26. Virgo		26. Scorp.	8:06 pm	26. Sagitt.	
27. Libra	2:47 am	27. Scorp.		27. Sagitt.	
28. Libra		28. Scorp.		28. Capric.	3:13 am
29. Scorp.	2:14 pm	29. Sagitt.	8:38 am	29. Capric.	
30. Scorp.		30. Sagitt.		30. Aquar.	2:20 pm
		31. Capric.	9:07 pm		

Summer time to be considered where applicable.

1999 MOON SIGN DATES—NEW YORK TIME

JULY Day Moon Enters		AUGUST Day Moon Enters		SEPTEMBER Day Moon Enters	
1. Aquar.		1. Aries	11:48 am	1. Taurus	
2. Pisces	11:35 pm	2. Aries		2. Gemini	0:26 am
3. Pisces		3. Taurus	4:10 am	3. Gemini	
4. Pisces		4. Taurus		4. Cancer	3:11 am
5. Aries	6:22 am	5. Gemini	6:58 pm	5. Cancer	
6. Aries		6. Gemini		6. Leo	6:30 am
7. Taurus	10:23 am	7. Cancer	8:54 pm	7. Leo	
8. Taurus		8. Cancer		8. Virgo	10:58 am
9. Gemini	0:01 pm	9. Leo	10:57 pm	9. Virgo	
10. Gemini		10. Leo		10. Libra	5:17 pm
11. Cancer	0:28 pm	11. Leo		11. Libra	
12. Cancer		12. Virgo	2:23 am	12. Libra	
13. Leo	1:27 pm	13. Virgo		13. Scorp.	2:09 am
14. Leo		14. Libra	8:25 am	14. Scorp.	
15. Virgo	4:40 pm	15. Libra		15. Sagitt.	1:36 pm
16. Virgo		16. Scorp.	5:41 pm	16. Sagitt.	
17. Libra	11:20 pm	17. Scorp.		17. Sagitt.	
18. Libra		18. Scorp.		18. Capric.	2:14 am
19. Libra		19. Sagitt.	5:33 am	19. Capric.	
20. Scorp.	9:31 am	20. Sagitt.		20. Aquar.	1:39 pm
21. Scorp.		21. Capric.	6:00 pm	21. Aquar.	
22. Sagitt.	9:49 pm	22. Capric.		22. Pisces	9:52 pm
23. Sagitt.		23. Capric.		23. Pisces	
24. Sagitt.		24. Aquar.	4:50 am	24. Pisces	
25. Capric.	10:09 am	25. Aquar.		25. Aries	2:35 am
26. Capric.		26. Pisces	0:51 pm	26. Aries	
27. Aquar.	8:55 pm	27. Pisces		27. Taurus	4:52 am
28. Aquar.		28. Aries	6:10 pm	28. Taurus	
29. Aquar.		29. Aries		29. Gemini	6:22 am
30. Pisces	5:28 am	30. Taurus	9:42 pm	30. Gemini	
31. Pisces		31. Taurus			

Summer time to be considered where applicable.

1999 MOON SIGN DATES—NEW YORK TIME

OCTOBER Day Moon Enters		NOVEMBER Day Moon Enters		DECEMBER Day Moon Enters	
1. Cancer	8:32 am	1. Virgo	11:08 pm	1. Libra	0:30 pm
2. Cancer		2. Virgo		2. Libra	
3. Leo	0:14 pm	3. Virgo		3. Scorp.	10:36 pm
4. Leo		4. Libra	6:58 am	4. Scorp.	
5. Virgo	5:41 pm	5. Libra		5. Scorp.	
6. Virgo		6. Scorp.	4:47 pm	6. Sagitt.	10:28 am
7. Virgo		7. Scorp.		7. Sagitt.	
8. Libra	0:53 am	8. Scorp.		8. Capric.	11:15 pm
9. Libra		9. Sagitt.	4:16 am	9. Capric.	
10. Scorp.	10:02 am	10. Sagitt.		10. Capric.	
11. Scorp.		11. Capric.	5:01 pm	11. Aquar.	12:00 pm
12. Sagitt.	9:20 pm	12. Capric.		12. Aquar.	
13. Sagitt.		13. Capric.		13. Pisces	11:19 pm
14. Sagitt.		14. Aquar.	5:47 am	14. Pisces	
15. Capric.	10:05 am	15. Aquar.		15. Pisces	
16. Capric.		16. Pisces	4:22 pm	16. Aries	7:31 am
17. Aquar.	10:18 pm	17. Pisces		17. Aries	
18. Aquar.		18. Aries	10:58 pm	18. Taurus	11:46 am
19. Aquar.		19. Aries		19. Taurus	
20. Pisces	7:34 am	20. Aries		20. Gemini	0:40 pm
21. Pisces		21. Taurus	1:27 am	21. Gemini	
22. Aries	0:42 pm	22. Taurus		22. Cancer	11:53 am
23. Aries		23. Gemini	1:15 am	23. Cancer	
24. Taurus	2:26 pm	24. Gemini		24. Leo	11:33 am
25. Taurus		25. Cancer	0:30 am	25. Leo	
26. Gemini	2:34 pm	26. Cancer		26. Virgo	1:35 pm
27. Gemini		27. Leo	1:20 am	27. Virgo	
28. Cancer	3:10 pm	28. Leo		28. Libra	7:15 pm
29. Cancer		29. Virgo	5:12 am	29. Libra	
30. Leo	5:48 pm	30. Virgo		30. Libra	
31. Leo				31. Scorp.	4:37 am

Summer time to be considered where applicable.

1999 FISHING GUIDE

	Good	Best
January	3-4-5-17-24-28-30-31	1-2-9-29
February	1-2-3-16-23-27-28	8
March	1-2-3-10-28-29-30	4-5-17-24-31
April	16-22	1-2-3-9-27-28-29-30
May	2-3-8-15-22-29-30-31	1-27-28
June	13-20-25-26-27-30	1-2-7-28-29
July	1-6-13-25-28-29-30	20-26-27-31
August	11-19-23-24-25-26-29	4-27-28
September	2-9-17-22-25-26	23-24-27-28
October	22-23-24-26-27-31	2-9-17-21-25
November	16-20-23-24-29	8-21-22-25-26
December	7-16-20-21-22-24-25	19-23

1999 PLANTING GUIDE

	Aboveground Crops	Root Crops
January	1-20-21-25-29	2-8-9-10-11-12-16
February	17-21-25-26	4-5-6-7-8-12-13
March	20-21-24-25-31	4-5-6-7-11-12-16
April	17-21-27-28-29	1-2-3-4-8-9-12-13
May	18-19-25-26-27-28	1-5-6-10-14
June	14-15-21-22-23-24	1-2-6-7-10-11-29
July	18-19-20-21-22-26-27	3-4-8-12-31
August	15-16-17-18-22-23	4-5-8-9-27-28-31
September	11-12-13-14-18-19-23-24	1-4-5-27-28
October	10-11-12-16-17-21	2-8-25-29-30
November	8-12-13-17-18-21-22	5-6-7-25-26
December	9-10-14-15-19	2-3-4-5-23-29-30-31

	Pruning	Weeds and Pests
January	2-11-12	4-5-6-7-13-14
February	7-8	1-2-3-9-10-14-15
March	6-7-16	2-9-10-14
April	3-4-12-13	5-6-10-11-15
May	1-10	2-3-7-8-12-30-31
June	6-7	4-5-8-9-12
July	3-4-12-31	1-2-6-10-29
August	8-9-27-28	2-6-7-10-29-30
September	4-5	2-3-7-8-9-26-30
October	2-29-30	4-5-6-7-27-31
November	7-25-26	1-2-3-23-24-27-28-29-30
December	4-5-23-31	7-25-26-27-28

1999 PHASES OF THE MOON—NEW YORK TIME

New Moon	First Quarter	Full Moon	Last Quarter
Dec. 18 ('98)	Dec. 26 ('98)	Jan. 1	Jan. 9
Jan. 17	Jan. 24	Jan. 31	Feb. 8
Feb. 16	Feb. 22	March 2	March 10
March 17	March 24	March 31	April 8
April 15	April 22	April 30	May 8
May 15	May 22	May 30	June 6
June 13	June 20	June 28	July 6
July 12	July 20	July 28	Aug. 4
Aug. 11	Aug. 18	Aug. 26	Sept. 2
Sept. 9	Sept. 17	Sept. 25	Oct. 1
Oct. 9	Oct. 17	Oct. 24	Oct. 31
Nov. 7	Nov. 16	Nov. 23	Nov. 29
Dec. 7	Dec. 15	Dec. 22	Dec. 29

Each phase of the Moon lasts approximately seven to eight days, during which the Moon's shape gradually changes as it comes out of one phase and goes into the next.

There will be a partial solar eclipse during the New Moon phase on February 16 and August 11.

There will be a lunar eclipse during the Full Moon phase on July 28.

Use the Moon phases to connect you with your lucky numbers for this year. See the next page (page 112) and your lucky numbers.

LUCKY NUMBERS
FOR CAPRICORN: 1999

Lucky numbers and astrology can be linked through
the movements of the Moon. Each phase of the thir-
teen Moon cycles vibrates with a sequence of numbers
for your Sign of the Zodiac over the course of the year.
Using your lucky numbers is a fun system that connects
you with tradition.

New Moon	First Quarter	Full Moon	Last Quarter
Dec. 18 ('98)	Dec. 26 ('98)	Jan. 1	Jan. 9
9 3 2 7	1 8 4 9	1 6 1 0	1 3 5 8
Jan. 17	Jan. 24	Jan. 31	Feb. 8
0 2 3 6	6 4 9 5	7 6 6 8	8 1 0 7
Feb. 16	Feb. 22	March 2	March 10
7 3 9 7	3 8 5 9	2 9 2 4	4 0 1 6
March 17	March 24	March 31	April 8
6 9 5 1	0 7 2 2	2 4 6 0	9 3 8 2
April 15	April 22	April 30	May 8
2 9 5 7	4 8 8 0	4 3 0 9	9 5 8 6
May 15	May 22	May 30	June 6
6 2 7 3	7 7 9 2	6 0 8 4	4 7 5 1
June 13	June 20	June 28	July 6
0 6 3 7	7 4 6 8	0 5 1 0	4 2 7 3
July 12	July 20	July 28	August 4
3 9 4 4	6 7 0 4	3 9 3 1	0 6 2 8
August 11	August 18	August 26	Sept. 2
8 3 3 5	5 7 0 8	8 7 5 1	0 6 3 7
Sept. 9	Sept. 17	Sept. 25	Oct. 1
7 7 9 2	2 0 8 5	2 6 2 7	7 4 8 8
Oct. 9	Oct. 17	Oct. 24	Oct. 31
8 1 3 0	6 9 5 2	9 5 1 7	7 2 2 4
Nov. 7	Nov. 16	Nov. 23	Nov. 29
4 6 0 3	3 8 2 3	5 4 1 0	5 5 7 9
Dec. 7	Dec. 15	Dec. 22	Dec. 29
9 3 6 2	2 5 3 4	1 9 6 0	1 0 3 5

CAPRICORN
YEARLY FORECAST: 1999

Forecast for 1999 Concerning Business
Prospects, Financial Affairs, Health,
Travel, Employment, Love and Marriage
for Persons Born with the Sun
in the Zodiacal Sign of Capricorn,
December 21–January 19.

This year promises to be an exciting and creative one for those of you born under the influence of the Sun in the zodiacal sign of Capricorn, whose ruler is Saturn, planet of form and duty. There will be more room to maneuver and develop individual artistic and creative abilities, both through work and independently. You are likely to be moving around more in the next twelve months, possibly changing your home as well as having more change in your day-to-day environment. Greater travel opportunities can lead to stronger business and social contacts being made, which can be especially helpful for you self-employed Capricorn men and women. Your perspective may become more far reaching as a result of this also. Your private and personal time is likely to become more important to you. Where business matters are concerned, it may be necessary to change direction quite significantly. It is possible that you will be shifting away from long-established alliances. This should provide opportunities to make productive new links. Keep an open mind in terms of where you can expand your business this year, since the most uncommon opportunities can turn out to be the most lucrative ones. Business partnerships may hinder more than help during the first part of the year, when you would prefer to have the freedom to act on your own initiatives. Try to be patient; it can be beneficial to have a partner to fall back on later in the year when the alliance can prove to be markedly profitable. Financially, it can be a year of marked ups and downs. Income from property investments may save the day during the more difficult periods. Your personal life and hobbies may be the reason for spending more money generally this year. In regard to health matters, you may need to guard against worrying too much about a partner's general well-being. The person may be stronger than you think when it comes to dealing with pressures and difficulties. Where travel is concerned, you may be busier with trips during the first few months of the year. This can be as a result of being eager to venture into fresh territory. There may be more reason generally for domestic travel than for trips to foreign destinations. Where routine occupational affairs are concerned, this can be a busier year. It can be important to pick and choose which commitments you take on, since there is a risk of becoming overloaded if you do not discriminate. In relation to matters of the heart, developing a lasting and fulfilling relationship is likely to be very important.

You professional Capricorn people may have difficulties in developing in the direction you want at the start of the year. This obstacle is probably alliances with business associates, who may be determined to keep to an established pattern. This should be a creative year in general, however. You are likely to have more room to maneuver once the first few months have passed. In order to gain more individual freedom, you may consider separating from one particular partner or associate in the long term. Making more effort to develop your contacts network this year can be worthwhile. It is possible that a number of fresh business opportunities will result. Unusual options to develop the business in a totally different direction may unfold. Do not be in too much of a hurry to expand too soon, though. Steady development can be preferable. There may be ways to use creative initiatives this year to improve the overall business profits or make more of assets. Training schemes may turn out to be more eye-opening than you expect. Visiting lecturers on schemes such as these can be a main source of valuable information which will influence the steps you take for the future. If you are interested in moving into new markets, consider youths and infants. Your budget may need careful attention during the first few months of the year, when expenditure is best kept to a minimum. The period between June 29 and August 24 is likely to be one of the most profitable of the year.

Where finances are concerned, do not depend on your situation remaining fixed over the next twelve months. It may be beneficial to have more than one source of income. For example, income from renting out property can be a useful mainstay during periods when your general financial security may dip. It may even be possible to increase rents by a small percentage this year, especially if improvements have been made. Aspects of your private life, particularly creative and romantic interests, can be more costly this year. It can be well worthwhile to invest in your talents, however, since you may be able to increase your career prospects by doing so. Your natural cautious streak is often a boon where money matters are concerned. Keep in touch with that side of your nature, regardless of how many outside interests you develop. It is possible that your income will fluctuate through changes taking place not just for yourself, but for fellow colleagues too. If you belong to a profit-sharing scheme, for example, the income from this may fall if the company has a bad year. Avoid committing yourself to ongoing, long-term expenditure, which could end up being too much of a drain on your resources. It will be

wise to cut back on spending during the period between March 18 and May 5, especially if you have major purchases to make or expenses to cover over the
summer months.

Where health matters are concerned, your partner's
circumstances may be of more mutual concern than
your own. He or she may have to work longer hours,
for example, with less time to relax and wind down. If
you are worried about this, it can start to have rever-
berations in your own health and well-being. It will
probably be wise to look for practical answers, rather
than to allow the situation to get to you. Do not un-
derestimate the power of mind over matter. If you find
it impossible to really relax, consider taking classes in
practices such as yoga or meditation, which will be supportive.

Travel opportunities are likely to abound this year,
especially during the first few months. Brief, regular
trips may take up a lot of your time. These may be
linked to expanding your social and business contacts.
As your everyday itinerary can be quite busy, you are
likely also to crave a complete breakaway. If you cannot afford the time for a proper vacation, weekend
breaks may be the answer. But try to find time for a
more lengthy getaway if you can. This can give you a
much clearer perspective on your entire situation. Time
spent away from the big city can be truly refreshing for
you Capricorn people who tend to spend many of your
waking hours in offices. If you want to plan ahead for
a summer vacation, the period between June 29 and
August 24 will be one of the most suitable.

Where routine occupational affairs are concerned,
your year is likely to be an active and demanding one.
Additional responsibilities may be foisted on you, and
you may not feel in a position to refuse them. Never-
theless, it will be wise to be realistic about what you
can practically manage. Especially if your partner's
time is already quite limited, it can be sensible not to

take on too many burdens yourself. This probably would not be mutually supportive from the point of view of handling routine tasks. The practical or procedural content of your job may change this year, due to an overall change in company policy.

Where marriage is concerned, it can be in your interests to avoid getting into a rut. The established routine of previous years may appeal to you less. Broadening your horizons is an experience which can be shared together and will probably enrich your relationship in the bargain. Travel and further educational interests alike can provide the right opportunities for expansion. The summer period can be especially rewarding, perhaps because you are able to fit in an exotic vacation. You single Capricorn men and women may be moving in the opposite direction in that you would perhaps appreciate greater structure and stability in the romantic area of your life. Part-time love affairs may not be enough to make you feel happy, even if your life is quite busy in other respects. If you have been involved in such a relationship for quite some time, this may be the year when you decide enough is enough. Either it must become permanent, or you will look farther afield for something more satisfying. It is likely that if the partnership area of your life is on an even keel, you will find other areas easier to handle. Therefore it will be worth holding out for the right person. This applies particularly to you attached Capricorn men and women, whose stable partnerships should be a boon this year.

CAPRICORN
DAILY FORECAST: 1999

1st Week/January 1–7

Friday January 1st. Those of you Capricorn people who do work at home are sure to be up to your neck in it already. You can also get down to tapping out letters on your personal computer or dealing with household matters. If you are busy studying for some course that helps you with your workaday life, you are likely to settle down to some serious and studious reading in a quiet corner at home.

Saturday the 2nd. Already you may feel that a relationship issue is becoming a problem. You seem to be arousing someone's wrath in a major way. Perhaps you need to be less cold and unbending. You will feel somewhat hurt and rejected by another person's attitude. A parent may be especially difficult to deal with, but you are sure to act dutifully if nothing else as you enter this new year.

Sunday the 3rd. The morning can see a continuation of your coldness and huffiness with someone. By the afternoon, you may be a trifle more forgiving. However, a confusing money matter can become a source of anxiety and worry. Taxes and insurance matters need to be dealt with carefully and honestly. Someone may be trying to cheat you out of your cash, so beware.

Monday the 4th. A source of income from some private work can really cheer you up. You may feel a bit better off and less thrown about by embarrassing bills and demands. Put your energies into your work and dealing with the public. You may hear some good news about an older person who is in the hospital. Writing a letter to parents or calling them on the phone can heal the breach.

Tuesday the 5th. Now your recent hard work can begin to pay dividends. But money seems to have a habit of dissolving like water just now. You may spend too much on presents and good times for a loved one. Unexpected news from abroad can cheer you up. But you may have to keep it a secret as yet. You tend to be thorough and disciplined about money matters, which can result in less worry for you.

Wednesday the 6th. Your strength of character will impress someone in an interview. A teacher or counselor may give you some praise off the cuff. You can get quite involved with private research work. This can take you to museums and archives to dig up information for your studies. The day is especially good for detailed work. Certain problems may occur while traveling.

Thursday the 7th. You may try to pack in a lot of courses or seminars. This can be because you are feeling a little lacking in confidence about a study matter. But don't give up just yet. It may simply be that you are overextending yourself. Try to see where you can cut back and make life simpler. You tend to be critical of in-laws, and they may be critical of you.

Weekly Summary

This will not be an easy week to start off your new year. A recent relationship problem may have been put aside over the Christmas period and a truce called for a while. But it can loom again when the Full Moon on Saturday makes you see just how bored you are with a certain partnership. Either you will feel rejected by another's coldness, or it may be coming from you. Either way, it's time to take a long, hard look at what is happening.

Take a look at your family or business finances this week. You may find that things have gotten into a bit of a muddle while you were away from work. You may have to correct other people's mistakes and careless errors. However, once this is done, you are sure to find that a certain private deal or investment is now paying off nicely and adding to your bank balance. But things are still a bit uncertain when it comes to regular earnings.

Those of you who are students need to beware of trying too many new things. You tend to overwork as it is. Keep life simple and try to be more philosophical.

2nd Week/January 8–14

Friday the 8th. Your attitude toward your career can be idealistic now. Your desire will be to help others less fortunate through what you do. However, try not to preach too much, or you will become annoying. An unexpected gift from a loved one can cheer you. Some new ways of investing your cash or a property deal may offer an exciting prospect and one that you should consider seriously.

Saturday the 9th. You are likely to be a bit heavy-handed with others you are working with this weekend. Your personal ambition can be carrying you ahead but at the cost of good relationships with staff or bosses. You may try to repress some feelings of annoyance and irritation. It will be much wiser to keep a low profile and let others choose their own paths.

Sunday the 10th. A somewhat cool reception at home may make you want to be back at work again. A parent or other family member can be playing hard to get along with. Later on you may feel a need to escape to a group whose company you enjoy. A spiritual friend also may be able to help. However, you need to be realistic about life and face what is going on if you are to make the most of this year.

Monday the 11th. Conversations of a serious sort should appeal to you most just now. You can experience a lot of love and friendship through a group of people you like being with. A brother or sister may have some demands to make on your purse. But you can be willing to help out if there is real need. This day can be good for meetings of a somewhat unconventional kind.

Tuesday the 12th. You probably will be quite expansive in regard to your social activities. This can be a very happy time for you. A loved one will be especially important to you now. You can really feel at ease with a certain friend with whom you can talk as you like. This will be a favorable day for all money matters. You can be delighted with the outcome of a private deal.

Wednesday the 13th. Your little sideline business schemes can be lucky and successful now, but things can rapidly change. You may find that dealing with gas, oil, or pharmaceutical matters is favorable. A loved one may tend to be fairly changeable of late. However, you seem to enjoy the challenge this creates. Unexpected bonuses or tax refunds can make you feel affluent and able to afford something special.

Thursday the 14th. You may want to surprise someone you know who is in a hospital. A visit to a loved one in a nursing home can be your good deed for the day. Being alone may be what you prize most; however, you may use your time to think of money matters all the time. Your gentleness and kindness can win you love from others. You should be feeling more caring in all aspects of your life.

Weekly Summary

There are times when you Capricorn people cannot wait to get back to work and to your normal routines. Holidays or home concerns can seem trying interludes for some of you. Many of you will be working weekends now to try to catch up or to make a bit of overtime pay. This weekend, however, you may feel very strained and tense about some development on the job front. Those of you who are looking for work may be let down and disappointed.

At least, you can be glad that your social life is better this week. You can really relax and enjoy yourself with a special group of people. A much loved friend may also be just the panacea you are looking for. In fact, you seem inclined to spend quite a lot on wining and dining someone you love. You tend to take a very calm and detached attitude toward all your social affairs and friendships just now.

Being alone is seldom a problem to you solitary-minded Capricorn people. You may spend some time reflecting, meditating, and doing yoga this week. Private little business deals can make you feel very good about yourself, especially on Thursday, when things go very well for you.

3rd Week/January 15–21

Friday the 15th. You are likely to be spending time alone working out various professional matters. Certain tasks may need doing about the house. You can attend to these in your usual organized and efficient fashion. You may have a wealth of ideas on how you want to spend your retirement. This can be a good time for making wills, dealing with inheritances, and so on, so that you can continue your present way of living.

Saturday the 16th. You need to make all your plans and ideas known to others. Don't keep hugging them to yourself. A boss or other superior seems to be on the warpath about something left undone. You will tend to be irritated and annoyed by someone's attitude at work. Watch out that ego clashes don't lead to a big row. Try to see the other person's viewpoint.

Sunday the 17th. This can be a day when you feel especially frustrated by family matters. Yet your attitude is likely to be philosophical and even cheerful. This can make it easier to cope with elderly people or trying relatives. You may feel a little tired, but there seems to be a lot to do about the house. Worries about work matters aren't likely to help much either.

Monday the 18th. This can be a time to straighten out your personal finances. Your private income may be very good now. However, you seem to have a completely uninterested approach to the whole business of making money. This may mean that others will con you or take advantage of you in some way. So don't opt out, but rather keep an eye out. Do not fall for dubious propositions.

Tuesday the 19th. Take some time to send flowers to a relative or buy nice things for the home. You may need to be on the good side of a family member now. You may feel a bit weary with the hard pace at work. Some of you seem to be losing your enthusiasm for a professional matter. However, you seem to be doing well enough financially to keep you from worrying too much.

Wednesday the 20th. It can be hard getting down to any studies. You may be deep in thought about some private or secret matters. This may be a time when some quite troubling situation makes you feel a little upset. News from someone who is sick at home or in the hospital may be a worry. Research work can be running up against a spot of trouble too. You may have to scrap a project.

Thursday the 21st. Having a chat with a partner can help you to make a few decisions or to finalize a plan. A good deal of the day may be spent on the phone, reading, or writing letters. You are likely to be quite chatty now, much to everyone's surprise. This will be a good day for giving lectures and talks. Local matters can be on your mind, and a neighbor may have something to tell you.

Weekly Summary

This can turn out to be a somewhat difficult time for pursuing personal goals and plans. But you will be quite determined and stubborn to boot and are likely to go ahead just the same. Your mind seems to be overflowing with good ideas, but maybe some of your ambitions are just a bit far-fetched or overoptimistic. This is unlike your usual cautious and pessimistic attitude.

Lately your financial life, although changeable and uneven, seems to be less of a burden or worry. This can be due to a more detached and spiritual attitude toward money. However, some of you might be acting somewhat erratically or even too laid-back. This can give those less scrupulous plenty of scope to cheat you or pull the wool over your eyes. Be detached by all means, but don't be foolish.

Some of you Capricorn people may be very busy working out various official matters for your local council or a comittee you belong to. You can be eager to bring out some proposals and ideas of your own that can help to improve and reform things. However, you may run up against some opposition here.

4th Week/January 22–28

Friday the 22nd. Now your brain seems to be teeming with bright ideas. Your general mood tends to be positive and cheerful. The morning can pass pleasantly chatting with a relative or a neighbor. Later in the day, you can spend time in the house, or the garden if you live in a warm climate. This can be a real escape from pressures, and you should feel relaxed.

Saturday the 23rd. Maybe it is time to have some major alteration made to the house. Or you can find yourself dealing with unexpected repairs. However, nothing seem to be too difficult for you to tackle. In fact, you are likely to feel a real sense of satisfaction from your efforts. You will enjoy the company of an uncle or a sibling, probably over dinner or a drink.

Sunday the 24th. Your tactfulness and charm are sure to win over a parent. You seem to be bent on pleasing someone, that's for sure. You can be busy with household jobs this morning and completely wrapped up in them. However, a neighbor may drop in, and the break can be welcome. Take care not to gossip too much. You may hear news that you find quite worrying later in the day.

Monday the 25th. This seems to be the sort of day when anything can happen. So be prepared for the unexpected. You will feel a little annoyed when a child acts in a rebellious or difficult fashion. Teachers may find it a particularly trying time for dealing with young folks. Although you may feel quite creative, your ideas seem too bizarre or scattered to have any really practical value.

Tuesday the 26th. Now it can be a lot easier than usual to get down to a hobby or creative pastime. It isn't easy to relax for some reason, but you appear to be a lot more cheerful and positive. You are likely to put your foot in it at work with a somewhat tactless remark. A lot of paperwork, filing, or phone calls can keep you busy; in fact, things can get pretty hectic.

Wednesday the 27th. Just getting on with routine paperwork, bills, and other daily matters can keep you occupied. You may be in the mood for a massive clearing out of all sorts of accumulated stuff. You may be a bit dreamy or preoccupied at times. A specific money matter seems to be on your mind. Take steps to get it straight, and don't be too vague about it all.

Thursday the 28th. Try not to take on too much or set yourself too many tasks. You can get a good deal done, as you are in a particularly efficient mood just now. The morning can be the best time for routine jobs. Later on, a mate or spouse may surprise you by arranging a pleasant dinner with the neighbors or taking you out for a drink or to a special concert or lecture.

Weekly Summary

On the whole, this should turn out to be a pleasant week for home and family matters. You can be more inclined than usual to be forgiving, thoughtful, and kindly toward your nearest and dearest. A less selfish or less coldly dutiful attitude certainly will help. This may be a time when certain repairs or reconstructions are necessary to the home or yard. You can enjoy working all this out and getting things shipshape again.

Those of you who deal with children through your work may find that they are likely to be troublesome. However, this can pass fairly soon, and you should be able to restore the kind of order you like. Parents may need to take a more good-humored and lenient view of a child's escapades. You need to remember that you were young once, although that's sometimes quite hard for you serious Capricorn people.

Daily and routine activities can mark the rest of this period. You can enjoy just attending quietly to the details and small knotty everyday problems that need to be solved. Be sure that any directions you give to a colleague at work are clear and not misunderstood.

5th Week/January 29–February 4

Friday the 29th. This is sure to be an interesting time for meeting a loved one. You can be very energetic and definite in stating your needs and desires. It is likely to be a time of intense and deep feeling for those in love. You may have to make an important decision about a neighborhood matter. A special function may need a lot of work and a good deal of organizing.

Saturday the 30th. This weekend can see you far happier in your relationship with your mate or spouse. But there still seems to be some coldness, resentment, or displeasure on someone's part that hits you hard. After all, you feel that you are trying hard to be kind. The evening can turn out to be on the argumentative side. A friend seems to be bearing some sort of grudge against you.

Sunday the 31st. You now seem to be getting a lot more anxious about both personal and joint finances. A completely unexpected development or an overlooked insurance bill can indicate that you are not as flush as you thought. It may mean having to spend extra time trying to sort out some kind of muddle or misunderstanding. You are unlikely to find an accountant sympathetic even if you can locate one on the weekend.

Monday February 1st. A parent may come to your rescue when it comes to settling a bill. There may be some cash to help you out in a private account. An inheritance or tax refund can be the saving of some of you. Escape from all these matters with a loved one tonight. You would have a pretty disappointing time with a group of friends, so you will be better off at home.

Tuesday the 2nd. Although you try hard to placate someone, you don't seem to succeed. It can be that others just have too many grumbles or grudges against you. A journey you take can go well enough, but you will not be in the mood to enjoy anything much. Even beautiful scenery can leave you untouched. Students may be finding the going tough, especially those who are starting new courses.

Wednesday the 3rd. You can be delighted by a sudden invitation to see a friend who is living abroad. A journey may run up against some surprise developments. However, you can enjoy the change and a bit of excitement. You may find that your detached and broadminded approach to a local matter helps get a clear perspective. Meetings of any kind are likely to be quite successful.

Thursday the 4th. You may expect a lot from a vacation or a day trip. In-laws can be overbearing at times. The afternoon can be spent near the seaside. The day is good for communications, especially with young people. A brother or sister may get in touch with you after a long absence. Teachers will be able to deal with their students more sensitively and sympathetically than usual.

Weekly Summary

Your feelings are not ever likely to be heated, as this isn't usually your way of dealing with others. But this week, you can feel deeply and intensely about someone in your life. So much so that you can even come out with it, and who knows what will happen then. You are more inclined to be open about what you feel now, and this should help any relationship. People aren't mind readers and need to be told.

Careful planning and cautious dealings can help you to get your mutual funds in order again this week. You need to stop being quite so vague about things and get the reins back in your hands again. Perhaps you have been too trusting in delegating business matters to another. If so, now is the time to get matters back under your own control. You can find that a parent is willing to help you out with a loan.

This can be a good time for an early vacation. You may be planning a trip to some far-off place and feel excited about it all. However, be prepared for surprising developments at the last minute. You may be going to meet others while traveling.

6th Week/February 5–11

Friday the 5th. You can feel very deeply about some-one you secretly love, but it may be hard for you to show that you care. Someone's jealousy or possessive-ness may be a problem now. You should be delighted with the outcome of some behind-the-scenes maneu-vering. This can mean a lot to you professionally. This can be a very good time for money matters, especially investments.

Saturday the 6th. Things tend to go somewhat slowly this weekend. This may be due to the fact that some official is nosing about in your business matters. You are likely to find that duties and responsibilities at home now interfere with your work plans. Remember-ing past happenings or looking over old family photos can make you a little sad at times. But some memories may bring a chuckle or even a guffaw.

Sunday the 7th. You can be deceiving yourself about a lover's feelings. Usually you are most realistic, if not cynical, but it can be hard to remain detached just now. A phone call or visit may bring disappointing news. You may regret having trusted a friend with your money. A sudden invitation to a neighborhood party can come when you least expect it and when you most need a break.

Monday the 8th. Although you do your best, you will not be in a socializing mood tonight. You may find it hard to keep up idle chatter at a party or dinner date. A leader in a group to which you belong may tend to be sarcastic. You can find a business meeting irritating and pointless. However, try not to let your irritation show too much. Calm down; it will all soon blow over.

Tuesday the 9th. This is likely to be a far more fortu-nate and positive day. You will feel much more in-clined to mix with others, especially in the morning. A group of foreigners can be fun to chat with. This can be a busy day, with many and varied activities. You can enjoy a little peace and quiet later on when you have more time to yourself. Perhaps you can watch that TV special.

Wednesday the 10th. You may delve deep into old records for a work you are interested in. This is a good time for those interested in writing, especially for the media. You may find it hard to relax; your mind seems to be occupied with all sorts of minor worries and anxieties. You may have to visit someone in a hospital, but can find the patient coming along nicely.

Thursday the 11th. A meeting that is held in private may need to be kept a secret just now. You may have dealings with various officials about foreign affairs. This can be a time when you will want to do some serious thinking and talking. A chat with an elderly person about the past can be most interesting. Those who are buying new cars or selling property should be able to get good deals.

Weekly Summary

You seem to lack your usual ambitious attitude toward your career these days. In fact, you may even feel downright bored with what you have no doubt been doing successfully for years. Maybe this is the time for a break or a change of some kind. You also can be feeling tired and harassed by home matters and duties there. These can take your attention away from your job. Try to get some rest and relaxation whenever possible.

Socially, you seem to have more going for you now. Group activities can be especially enjoyable if these have some spiritual content. You may be interested in helping out those who are less fortunate now. Your friendships will be likely to be with serious-thinking people who have a lot of commitment to such matters.

However, a group leader may tend to irritate you by being too self-righteous.

Spending some time alone during the week can be quite blissful once you get used to it. At first you may miss a loved one who has gone away for a while. Some of you may be involved with people in hospitals or homes just now. A lot of plans seem to be afoot to help raise cash for such places.

7th Week/February 12–18

Friday the 12th. Arranging a special function can use up a lot of energy. However, you are sure to get everything well organized and ready in time. You seem determined to achieve certain very personal goals and will keep going until they are dealt with. A decision made now can affect a friend or a group with whom you are involved at present. By evening you will be ready for a good book or some television.

Saturday the 13th. A tender and gentle person can have a wonderful conversation with you. Now you are sure to feel very much more even-tempered and harmonious. In fact, your mood will be sensitive and caring for those in need. For once, you can stop being quite so stiff about life and relax a little. Dealings with neighbors will be cordial and may lead to plans for a party.

Sunday the 14th. You seem to be quite put out by a difficult family situation. An elderly person may annoy you this morning. You may act very dutifully but somewhat coldly. Try not to be too depressed by past mistakes. Things will cheer up by the afternoon. You may feel better tempered and more resigned to what needs to be dealt with. Be sure to be extra nice to your love this Valentine's Day.

Monday the 15th. Tax refunds, insurance settlements, or an inheritance can add considerably to your personal bank balance. You can find that a private job or a secret deal is now paying off. It is a good day for those who have to buy in bulk for a business. It also is favorable for planning your dealings in stocks, but take care when selling them off. You can feel a lot more lively and eager to find bargains while shopping.

Tuesday the 16th. It is time now for some kind of new start. This can mean a change of residence for some of you. You tend to cling to what you are used to, if only for mere convenience. But now you seem to be ready to make a very important decision that can affect a group of people in your life. You may test out a new car in your local area. After some negotiation, you probably will decide to buy it.

Wednesday the 17th. You may feel a need to say exactly what is on your mind. A group of people may seem to need reshuffling in some way. Your involvement with political matters will have to be kept under wraps. Try to take care that all you do is aboveboard, or you may have a brush with the law. Social activities, especially local ones, will be fun and may produce new friendships.

Thursday the 18th. Pleasant meetings and morning coffee hours with local friends can make the time pass enjoyably. You will feel a lot happier at home. It can be good to have some time to yourself. You may decide to redecorate or to contract for an extension to the home. A cautious and careful approach to money matters is likely to be best, but be sure that all bills are paid on time.

Weekly Summary

You are likely to feel good about yourself at the start of this week. Your charm and tenderness can go a long way toward making your loved ones respond with more feeling. You can be more interested now in the way you look and speak and may decide to buy some new clothes. Never one to be noisy, your calm and quiet speech can be very effective and have a stronger influence on others than you may realize.

This is likely to be a mixed week for money matters. However, on the whole, you will feel that you are coping quite well. In fact, with care, you can do quite nicely in the money markets, or sense the right things to buy for a business. Unexpected payments or rebates can also help considerably with your personal account. This can be a good time to spend some cash on home improvements.

Neighborhood matters may be of more importance and interest to you than usual. You can be on very good terms with those next door. In fact, for some of you, a local romance may be developing. It seems that quite a good deal is going on socially around you.

8th Week/February 19–25

Friday the 19th. This is a good time to get going on repairs at home. You may be making a few major changes to the home and rebuilding some of it. For those dealing in real estate, this can be an important time. You need to be ready to move in and buy things up at the right moment. A family friend may have a surprise in store for you. It can have something to do with a special day in your life.

Saturday the 20th. Be extra careful when negotiating a deal of some kind. You can find that others are not as honest as you thought. You may tend to be a bit of an escapist and lazy. However, if you can take some time to get away and enjoy a hobby or favorite sport, do so. Your dealings with children can be difficult, perhaps because you are a bit short on patience.

Sunday the 21st. Although a lot of social activities are going on just now, you seem to be lacking in energy or interest. In fact, certain activities or groups of people may make you feel quite wound up at the end of the day. It will be better to enjoy yourself with a lover. A quick phone call can change the whole mood of the day. Children can be irritating and noisy.

Monday the 22nd. A lot of daily and routine work can be achieved. You can really enjoy being at home just now. Getting on with decorating and making the place look good can make you feel good too. This is a favorable time to do some home entertaining. Cooking delicious dishes can be fun. A party for a loved one should go very well. The company and the food will be top-notch.

Tuesday the 23rd. The details of an accounting matter may need to be dealt with. You may have some problems with a child's teacher or a coach. In fact, take care that a tense ego confrontation doesn't occur. You are likely to come off the worst for it. However, if you use your own brand of charm and persuasiveness, you can make sure things move in the direction you want.

Wednesday the 24th. A more compassionate approach toward a parent is the best thing. You will feel a lot warmer and more loving toward the family in general. Try to be less irritable or sorry for yourself if you are not feeling well. You can be sure someone you least expect will care for you. You may find that your car is acting up and needs a visit to the repair shop.

Thursday the 25th. Don't overdo the charm with a mate or spouse or the person may suspect your sincerity. You can be too ingratiating with all those around you. However, much of this is due to your genuine kindness and sympathy. A neighbor will be glad of your help. Don't try to do all your decorating in one go, or you may make a careless mistake that will take a long time to remedy.

Weekly Summary

If you have to deal with children, your own or those of other people, this can be a tricky week. Youngsters tend to be noisy, rude, and rebellious at times whatever their age. However, try to remain detached and be sensitive to what is going on and what they need. A good talk can help to clear the air. This will not be an easy week for creative work or hobbies. You are likely to be impatient and may find concentration difficult.

Daily activities can keep you busy now. You may have a lot of extra cooking to do this week if you are filling up the freezer or planning to do home entertaining. You should be enjoying very pleasant relations with staff and co-workers this week. This can make the routine of each day a good deal easier to bear and far more cheerful. Machinery can break down occasionally and make life difficult.

You seem determined to try to please this week, but you may end up pleasing no one. Be sure that your motives are sincere when buttering others up. If you are being too calculating or manipulative, others will sense it and back off. Ego conflicts can make it hard to get along with a partner.

9th Week/February 26–March 4

Friday the 26th. This is likely to be a pleasant, light, and chatty day. You can enjoy conversations with a mate or spouse. A relative will be very kindly and sympathetic about your problems. Meetings with a legal representative should go well. You can get down to making neglected phone calls, writing letters, or just relaxing with your mate before the TV.

Saturday the 27th. Things may go much too slowly this morning. You can feel a little hurt by a partner's sudden cold attitude. Your deep need for sympathy may make you too sensitive. The afternoon or evening can be a lot more positive and cheerful. A really special friend will make you feel good. Group activities in your home can be fun and bring surprising results.

Sunday the 28th. A sudden change in your joint finances can be upsetting or disconcerting. You may have to get down to keeping track of the accounts for yourself. It can turn out to be a very tense day. You may be feeling stressed out by some quite unimportant matter. Try not to dramatize things too much. A sarcastic remark can get you in trouble.

Monday March 1st. A carefully planned journey can now take place. You may have to deal with an official about a study matter. You can feel somewhat powerless when it comes to a group situation. It seems that certain decisions have been made behind your back. You are likely to have to repress a lot of anger. However, a philosophical and practical approach can help work things out.

Tuesday the 2nd. Things can tend to get a bit out of your control. You can run up against some problems with a teacher if you are a student. For those of you with a lot of determination, however, this should be a good day for forging ahead with your research work and other interests. If you are traveling, you may encounter obstacles, but these can simply spur you on.

Wednesday the 3rd. Some angry or irritable words can make both home life and work uncomfortable. You may spend a good deal of time gossiping instead of getting on with your job. A brother or sister can get on your nerves. You may find yourself racing about all over the place giving people lifts. This can mean precious time wasted, but it will be much appreciated by these people.

Thursday the 4th. Money made now can be used for charitable donations. Family matters may still weigh heavily on your mind. However, you probably will decide that it is best to keep on good terms with everyone and not create any waves. You may feel annoyed about something you have bought for the house but no longer like. Maybe you can return or exchange it if you act quickly enough.

Weekly Summary

Now may be a good time to change a mortgage, insurance policy, or work out other ways of saving money. You can find this a very important week for business and family finances. Take stock of where you are now. It can be time to consider reinvesting your money or taking on new partners or staff. With some thought, you can cut a few corners now and help to get things moving along smoothly again.

This can be a fairly difficult time for you Capricorn students. You seem to be having troubles with teachers who seem capable of making you feel powerless or hopeless. However, you also appear to have a good deal of determination and courage. This can help you to pick up again and show others just what you are made of. On the whole, your self-discipline is good. In fact, you may drive yourself just a little bit too hard at times.

Your more ambitious nature is still under wraps for the present. You seem to be inclined to spend more time on the phone or doodling on your scratch pad than to face what needs to be done. Maybe this is due to the fact that your mind is occupied with problems at home.

10th Week/March 5–11

Friday the 5th. This can be a day full of surprises. You may be delighted with a special meal prepared just to please you. Family matters now seem much more harmonious. A friend may repay a debt now. Generally this will be a good time for making money; you can find that business is booming right now. A surprise visit from a loved one can be delightful. You will enjoy sharing news.

Saturday the 6th. A work situation may mean that you have to cancel a date tonight. Naturally this can be disappointing. However, you are in a self-sacrificing mood. It may be that you have to look after someone who is unwell and needs your attention. You may give some cash away to help an elderly person in trouble. A formal function can be very boring, so try to skip it if you can.

Sunday the 7th. Lively group discussions can be interesting but a bit upsetting at times. You should try to keep out of any dramatic rows or disagreements. You seem to have something hidden up your sleeve just now. A brother or sister may have confided something in you and asked you to keep quiet about it. A sudden decision can upset your desires and your plans.

Monday the 8th. This is likely to turn out to be a quite dull and ordinary kind of day. However, you aren't likely to mind that. In fact, for some of you it can provide a welcome rest from some recent ups and downs. As long as you can work hard and achieve plenty, you are sure to enjoy the day. You may see a special friend tonight, someone you have not seen for a long time.

Tuesday the 9th. A retreat or quiet evening can be good for you. You may want to spend some time in contemplation or meditation. Other pursuits such as yoga, tai chi, or prayer can also appeal just now. You can enjoy reading a voluminous and interesting book that grabs your attention. Being surrounded by family will make you feel comfortable and safe. Contentment will be your lot.

Wednesday the 10th. It should be relaxing to be at home surrounded by loved ones, but for some reason you seem to feel ill at ease with yourself. This can be caused by various private thoughts that are bothering you. If you have some sort of secret, it may be a good idea to find a friend you can confide in. You may enjoy cooking or cleaning in preparation for guests.

Thursday the 11th. This can be a quite disciplined and useful day. You may feel very organized and practical and can get a good deal done on a favorite hobby. This can require a lot of time and patience. However, it also can mean neglecting various things you need to do at home or at work. Paperwork especially seems to be piling up. Try to get something done before it gets out of hand.

Weekly Summary

Although you will have a few social invitations, you may be lacking in desire to get out and have a good time. In fact, you seem a little world-weary at times. However, an outing can restore your spirits and make you feel a lot more perky again. Friends you have known for years may suddenly appear boring or dull. But it is more likely that you are just seeing life too cynically.

Because of the mood you are in just now, you may decide to go on a retreat of some sort. This can certainly give you a more detached or spiritual perspective on things again. If this is not possible, try to get some time to yourself to contemplate and think things through in peace. On the whole, you Capricorn people enjoy such moments alone, but it can also be good to spend private time with a loved one.

Serious or practical hobbies and pleasures can make you happy at the end of this week. You can do things that are purely personal and enjoyable and feel that you are your own master. It may be that you are getting a little time to yourself if family members are visiting elsewhere.

11th Week/March 12–18

Friday the 12th. You seem to be a lot more goal-oriented and more like your old self. In fact, all your energies at present can be directed toward achieving some very personal ambition. This is sure to be good when you are so determined to succeed. A relative may get in touch with you. The person may have some quite unusual and very surprising news for you.

Saturday the 13th. You are likely to be quite irritated by a loved one this morning. Someone in the family seems to be in a very uncooperative mood just now. Such an attitude can be depressing when you feel you have tried so hard to please. But don't get too sorry for yourself. A debt may now need to be paid off just when you are broke; you may be chasing around in search of funds.

Sunday the 14th. You may feel really lucky now. This can be a good time to go through any retirement plans or insurance policies. In fact, older Capricorns will find this a time to make plans for a new home, perhaps in the country. You can get quite annoyed with people in a group to which you belong, especially if you notice they keep changing their tune.

Monday the 15th. This is likely to be a very favorable time for making money on a property deal. You can enjoy spending extra on beautifying the home or yard. Your more detached but warmer attitude can make a loved one more cooperative. It should be a harmonious day for family matters. You can relax a good deal more now in your own environment. If you need a bit of solitude, you can have it.

Tuesday the 16th. On the whole, your creativity tends at the best of times to be of the practical kind. So this can be a good day to do some woodwork, dressmaking, or other hobby with a useful or marketable end result. You may feel a bit frustrated by a neighbor disturbing your solitude and peace. But you need to do a little socializing too, so be gracious and welcome the interruption.

Wednesday the 17th. This can be a favorable time for beginning some new venture. You may be able to start a thesis or other writing project. Now you can feel comfortable with yourself. This should help to promote better relations with a mate or spouse. You can become involved in some local matter. Perhaps your interest will be in education or committees that help to improve facilities.

Thursday the 18th. It may be fun recalling past incidents and looking at old family photos. You can find that a family reunion is a very happy occasion. It will offer a chance to meet a brother or sister who has come to see you from overseas. Money matters are in good shape now, especially when a little private deal comes to a successful conclusion.

Weekly Summary

You keep pretty quiet about your feelings and reactions most of the time. In fact, at times it can be hard to know just what is going on in your head. However, it may be useful to be honest and not too secretive this week. Your goals seem to include getting a little peace and quiet just for yourself. This is sensible, for you can probably do with a break from too much pressure

This is likely to be a particularly rewarding week for money matters. You own account seems to be growing nicely thanks to a few little behind-the-scenes deals and some wheeling and dealing. But it may also be thanks to your prudence in providing insurance and other income for your retirement. Now you older Capricorn people can be cashing in on the thriftiness of your youth.

Many of you will be getting more involved in neighborhood matters now. You enjoy committee meetings and helping to get things organized. This can apply to running local senior citizen's clubs, helping out with educational matters for your children, and so on. It can be a favorable time to start such interests and to get them established.

12th Week/March 19–25

Friday the 19th. It is possible that some of you feel ready for a change of home or neighborhood. This can be a good time to discuss it with a mate or spouse. A real estate matter should be doing well. However, you may need to make some changes to a document or agreement. Meetings concerning local activities will be lively but will produce good results.

Saturday the 20th. You can achieve a great deal just now, which can give you a lot of satisfaction. However, it means having to put a lot of time and effort into various schemes, hobbies, or creative interests. But you are never one to shirk a little bit of hard work. You may be concerned about a child's educational prospects. Learn all you can about your local school district.

Sunday the 21st. Something can go wrong and mess up your best intentions. You may find yourself arguing with a neighbor about some trivial matter. A creative effort may not turn out as well as you hoped. Perhaps you are being too exacting with yourself. A child may be a source of some anxiety or disillusionment. Perhaps the child is running with the wrong crowd.

Monday the 22nd. Your need to get on with daily tasks can be strong. You may feel that you really need to have a massive clearing out of rubbish, or a regular spring cleaning. This can be a pleasant time for such matters, and you will feel very virtuous when all is done. Send your excess or unwanted goods to a thrift shop run by your favorite charity and feel even more angelic.

Tuesday the 23rd. Although unexpected developments may disturb your day, this can be a time for getting ahead with the nitty-gritty of routine work at home or in the office. You may have a lot of paperwork to catch up on, calls to make, and so on. Try not to waste too much time in gossip with colleagues or staff. Your nerves may not be too good, and you can be a bit jumpy.

Wednesday the 24th. You will be happy to see an old lover again. This can be a good time for dealing with older children who may need some wise advice. You can help out with their career matters if you are a teacher or social worker. A mate or spouse will seem a lot more caring and sympathetic. You should enjoy helping various local charitable activities achieve their goal.

Thursday the 25th. A lively discussion with a partner can be very helpful and constructive. A meeting of partners or shareholders also can do well. The day is good for social functions and special events. A mate or spouse may have some penetrating comments to make about certain mutual friends. You will be wise to listen and make notes for future reference.

Weekly Summary

This will be a good time for those of you who are in a creative mood. You are likely to want to make or enjoy only those things that seem to have a purpose. There is little time for anything frivolous in your life just now. If you go to theatrical events, you are likely to pick serious or classical programs. However, this is the way you Capricorn people have fun, and that is what counts in the end.

Make this your week for having a clearing out at home and in the workplace. This can be very good for you and give a sense of having cleared out inner problems as well. Generally it will be a favorable time for work matters of a commonplace kind. You can get on well with workmates or staff now. You seem inclined to discuss both your problems and those of others, which may be something of a waste of time.

Your partners in business or in love seem to be in accord with you this week. You can be much more sensitive and yet detached too. This can help when important matters need to be discussed between you. Generally it will be a very good time for relationship matters.

13th Week/March 26–April 1

Friday the 26th. You may find yourself unwilling to take a risk on a business matter. Your tendency to play safe can mean that you lose an opportunity. However, it is better to be safe than sorry, a motto that seems to have been written especially for you Capricorn people. You can feel quite anxious about a child. You may feel that the youngster's concentration is not as good as it could be.

Saturday the 27th. This can be a very cheerful and positive day for financial matters. You may find that interest has accumulated on some little venture. Or you may benefit from an inheritance or tax refund. You may find that a social event does not live up to its promise. A friend can let you down at the last minute and disrupt an evening's arrangements. Try not to get too angry.

Sunday the 28th. If you plan a journey with care, you can avoid delays. You may feel duty-bound to go to visit your in-laws. Students should find it easier to buckle down to their work. You can get a little upset over a loved one's tactless or sarcastic comments. However, you are unlikely to show how you feel no matter how much it hurts; your pride will not let you.

Monday the 29th. Your best bet now is to get off on a trip or a little spring break. You can find that a group of people are trying to involve you in political matters. You are likely to take a more tolerant or broad-minded view of things just now. Some of you may be having an extension or repair job done on the home. It can help create a good deal more living space.

Tuesday the 30th. This is not likely to be a very good time to travel. Driving can be hazardous because of weather conditions. Or you may find that you lose your way for some reason. You will be in a very absorbed and thoughtful mood. A book you are reading can really capture your attention and give you a means of escape from ordinary life. Traveling salespeople may feel frustrated and tired.

Wednesday the 31st. If you can resolve a few problems at work, things may begin to look a lot clearer. You probably will be doing a good many favors for others just now. This may be very noble of you but might not be good for business. A lover can be trying to break up a relationship. Naturally this will make you feel upset and worried, especially if you suspect there is someone else.

Thursday April 1st. You may be agreeably surprised by a neighbor's attitude. It can be a very lucky day for family events. In fact, some of you Capricorn people may be celebrating a special occasion such as Passover or a wedding anniversary or a christening in the family.

It can be a good day for professional matters. A boss is likely to be pleased with your efforts.

Weekly Summary

This week is sure to find you busily working on joint accounts and dealing with other people's money in various ways. In fact, you seem to be following up a few tips when it comes to investments. Your more cautious streak may hold you back at the last minute. However, it usually is wise to follow your instinct in such matters. Saturday is likely to be a lucky day when it comes to finances.

The week will be good for travel and for taking a break as long as you take care on the roads. Make sure that you get your car checked over before you make a long trip. Tuesday can be an especially irritating day for those on the road. You may long to find a little retreat somewhere where you can stay with a loved one. It can do you a world of good to get away and broaden your horizons with new faces and places.

Professionally speaking, this is sure to be your lucky week. You can exude a lot more confidence in yourself than usual. Naturally, this makes a good impression on customers and bosses alike. You need to be ready to take up any new opportunities and developments.

14th Week/April 2–8

Friday the 2nd. Older people in a group to which you belong may be a trifle annoying. You can feel disappointed in a theatrical performance. This is not a very good time for social activities. Things can take a lot of hard work organizing and then not turn out as you planned. You may feel quite hard and unforgiving toward an old friend who you find has gone over to the opposition.

Saturday the 3rd. This can be a time when surprise events take over. You can find you get a bit hot under the collar when you're with a group of people. Their stubborn and difficult attitude can really make you seethe. A social function may end up being very expensive and not really worth the trouble involved. Take care not to have a quarrel with a friend.

Sunday the 4th. A lover may phone you this Easter Sunday or send a message through a friend. This can unsettle you but also make you feel pleased. A meeting you attend concerning traffic or educational matters should be useful. You may enjoy reading some spiritual, medical, or romantic books. Too much to eat at a holiday dinner can upset your stomach, so go easy on the goodies.

Monday the 5th. This is a good time for spiritual activities. You probably are getting deeper into books or research on such matters. You can enjoy being alone to do some meditation or yoga. Your mind may be on a loved one. You can feel tenderly about such a person. An in-law can be gracious and charming now. Conversations about life are sure to be instructive, but just being in agreement will be enough.

Tuesday the 6th. You are sure to feel expansive and relaxed if you are on your own for a change. But at the same time, you can really miss a loved one who may have gone off for a while. Those who are now retired may be really enjoying all the extra time. The time is good for dealings in investments and real estate. You can meet a quite unusual person who may give you a few tips about your finances.

Wednesday the 7th. Your faith in a lover will now be restored. You can be glad to see someone you rely upon who supports you. An older child can be very dependable just now. This can be a good time to listen to serious music, see a classical play, or other such enjoyments. You may feel creative and be ambitious to excel at whatever you tackle, however difficult the task may be.

Thursday the 8th. Personal desires may seem a bit selfish. But you do need to please yourself as well as others occasionally. So make this a day on which you go where you like and do what you like. It can be good to enjoy your home and own environment. Maybe you now appreciate these things a great deal more than before. A family friend may call and come to see you with interesting news.

Weekly Summary

You seem to have a lot to cope with on the social scene this week. It may be that you have become involved in too many functions that need to be organized. Naturally, this can take a lot out of you, especially as you tend to want to get every detail just right. Try not to make life too burdensome. Friends or groups of people do seem to expect too much of you at times.

After a hectic weekend, you will be very glad to relax on your own. Even if you are at work, you seem to be able to get some time to yourself for a day or two. You can enjoy using such moments to catch up on spiritual reading or to do some meditation. Those of you who are involved in hospital or prison visiting may take on these kinds of duty this week. But try to relax a little as well.

Now it can be time for you to have some fun and deal with your own personal needs and pleasure. This may mean seeing someone you love to be with, someone who makes you feel comfortable and safe. Or you may prefer to be quite on your own and do nothing at all.

15th Week/April 9–15

Friday the 9th. A dose of parental disapproval can make you feel a little down in the mouth. You are likely to have some sort of ego clash with a family member. A very special person from your past may turn up. You can enjoy thinking about an old love affair or a meeting with a long-standing lover. Personal plans can be put into action now with the support of family members.

Saturday the 10th. You seem to have come to grips with a financial puzzle. It can be a slightly worrying time for you where money matters are concerned. Debts or official demands can make you feel restricted and held back. Take advantage of any overtime that comes your way. A formal social function can prove very boring and dull. You may want to skip it.

Sunday the 11th. This ought to be a more lucky day for you where making money is concerned. A sudden influx of cash can be promised from a special assignment. Or you may have a lucky win playing cards, winning a raffle, and so on. Prospects for selling or buying real estate are looking up. You may spend a fair amount at a garden center early in the day. Garden supplies and trays of herbs will interest you.

Monday the 12th. A gift for a loved one may not be appreciated. This can be quite upsetting. The afternoon seems to be a lot happier. You can shrug off annoyances and enjoy some serious reading or listen to favorite music. In fact, a concert will be inspiring for some of you. Take some time to enjoy a spot of golf or whatever sport you enjoy. You will not lack for companionship.

Tuesday the 13th. This is not likely to be a very easy day for teachers or students. You can feel slightly sluggish and not interested in what you're doing. Some of you may be a little disturbed by news you hear now, especially if it concerns a relative. A neighbor may be acting in a rough and noisy manner. But if you are wise, you will ignore this and keep out of trouble.

Wednesday the 14th. A good talk with other neighbors can be helpful this morning. You may be involved in drawing up petitions or organizing local meetings. Later in the day, you will be more inclined to relax in the home or yard. This can be a good time to concentrate on cooking or dressmaking. A party at home can be great fun. Invite local friends to meet relatives and others from out of town.

Thursday the 15th. Repairing the house can be important and really necessary. For once you can be in the mood to get on with it all determinedly and thoroughly. An unexpected call from a relative or local friend can please you. This will be a favorable time for those buying houses or furnishings for the home. You will be delighted with any recent changes you have made to the garden and house exterior.

Weekly Summary

If you have been putting off clearing a debt, it can surface with a vengeance this week. In fact, you may have to dig into your personal income to support a problematic hitch in your business. But at the same time, other sources of income can produce sudden and unexpected gains. You may benefit from a tax refund, inheritance, or other unplanned income. Dealing with red tape and officials can make things irritating, though.

You tend to be quite philosophical and serious in your communications just now. This will be a good time for those engaged in some quite demanding writing. You apparently have the discipline and organization necessary to get the task done. It can be pretty slow and painstaking work, but this seems to suit your temperament. Lectures or talks you give or attend are likely to be on conventional or classical subjects.

Dealing with home matters can be pleasant just now. You are sure to find family relationships more harmonious and relaxed. It may seem at times as if a real transformation has taken place in everyone's attitude toward each other. A great deal of this can be due to having more space to move in.

16th Week/April 16–22

Friday the 16th. You and a parent will be in real agreement about a family matter. You tend to feel more comfortable and at ease with yourself and others now. The morning can be a fortunate time for those moving to a new home. A new start in a new place can be just what is needed. The afternoon can get a bit chaotic at times. You may try to do too much and feel exhausted. Take a short break.

Saturday the 17th. It isn't always easy to cope with too talkative and rebellious youngsters. The day can see you getting tense and irritable when unexpected teenagers drop in and make too much noise and commotion. It will not be an easy time for creative matters. You may find it hard to come up with original ideas. A friend may be very excitable and strange. No one can figure out the reason.

Sunday the 18th. Plans may be afoot to add a new pet to your household. You may decide to go in for something quite unusual. This is likely to be a very pleasant day even though it can be simple and quiet. You can really feel a sense of peace from dealing with routine daily affairs. Spending time on the details of cooking, cleaning, and other mundane matters can be soothing for you.

Monday the 19th. A regular clearing out at home and in the office may unearth all sorts of lost items. You can have good relationships with your staff or colleagues. This can be a good time to consider asking for a pay raise. You are sure to enjoy the company of relatives who may have come from abroad. Your health can be a lot better now, thanks to some special treatment you have been undergoing.

Tuesday the 20th. Be careful not to spread any family gossip. You cannot be sure whose ears it is likely to reach. An older child may tend to be quite difficult. You probably will have to restrain your temper. But using sarcasm isn't going to be too helpful either. You may feel very tired and not in the mood for a social event tonight, so stay home and read or watch TV.

Wednesday the 21st. It will not be easy now to keep your feelings in bounds. It may turn out to be a very emotional time for family reunions. Your feelings can be very intense and deep. Something you eat is likely to disagree with you. You may get some helpful medical advice from a brother or sister. A delightful small pet can cheer you up, as can the antics of young children.

Thursday the 22nd. A bank manager or accountant is likely to be unsympathetic toward your problems. You may feel that a child is entirely too demanding these days. Trying to straighten out various investments or a recent little gamble may leave you feeling quite worried or confused. This is not a good time for socializing either; you can feel too irritable to be pleasant company.

Weekly Summary

Events are likely to move really fast this week. At the start of this period, you may find that an older child's needs or problems take up a lot of time. You will be very worried if children are acting oddly. Naturally, all sorts of ideas can present themselves to your mind. But don't act in a precipitate manner. Try to talk things through before making any judgments.

Everyday happenings and activities can be soothing to your soul. You Capricorn people never mind hard work. In fact, you tend to see it as a panacea for all ills. This can be a good time for those who enjoy dealing with detailed activities. Your relationships with people at work can be delightful and harmonious now, which certainly makes your daily routine much happier.

A partner seems to be making some pretty outrageous demands and behaving in an extravagant manner. This kind of thing can make you feel both bothered and irritated. However, don't let your anger simmer too long. It will be better to speak your mind out straight than to indulge in bitterness or sarcasm.

17th Week/April 23–29

Friday the 23rd. A meeting on business and financial matters can help clear up a lot. But you still seem to be worried and unsure about things. The sale of a house or other property can now come to fruition and make a big difference to you financially. Maybe you will be able to plow some back into your business. You seem to have a lot of plans in the pipeline and want to start quickly on them.

Saturday the 24th. Don't get drawn into doing things for a group out of feelings of guilt. You probably do more than your share already. You may feel tired and lacking in bounce. A friend may make you very angry, but it seems you cannot be bothered to retaliate. This can be a tough time for those who are dealing with handicapped children. Public help may not be forthcoming.

Sunday the 25th. A social occasion at college or school can be lively and enjoyable. You and a principal or other authority figure can have a lot to discuss. If you are dealing with handicapped or troublesome youngsters, you may have to call in help. The day will be good for travelers. You are likely to have to combine business as well as pleasure on a trip you make.

Monday the 26th. Making or buying clothes for a trip can save a lot of money. You may find yourself feeling unwell while away from home. Be sure to take any medicines you might need. A relative may have news that can change a good many things in your life. Daily activities can be disrupted, but this may prove more of a stimulant than an annoyance. It can give you time to clarify your thinking.

Tuesday the 27th. You probably will feel a little sorry for a family member. Your professional life may include having to deal with other people's finances. This can be a good time to clear up various matters that have been troubling you. You can feel more in control if teaching children or caring for young people with problems. They trust you and turn to you instinctively.

Wednesday the 28th. Various major changes in your professional life can be a bit hard to get used to at first. You may find it hard to put across certain ideas to your clients or boss. However, you seem to be keeping calm, and this can be very helpful when dealing with others who are stressed out. Don't try to do too much in one day. In most cases, everything can be put off for a few days.

Thursday the 29th. This can be a very intense and concentrated day for many of you. A group of people you meet tonight may have a transforming impact on you. It may be very hard to keep up a show of interest when at a professional function. Your mind tends to be on deeper matters altogether. Political or radical interests can become really obsessive, but the people you meet will not share your concerns.

Weekly Summary

Don't let business finances preoccupy you to the exclusion of all else. All work and no play can make any Capricorn person dull. You can be sure of only one thing as far as joint finances go; nothing seems to be stable or certain. So live for today and don't worry too much. You may have a really unexpected windfall this week. But equally, you may get a bill that completely stuns you.

It isn't the best time to go on your travels, but for some of you who are students or teachers, it can now be the start of a new term. This may mean traveling back to your college or school. En route you may find yourself with a group of people who are highly entertaining and interesting. At least, this can make a slow journey pass more quickly. You may have to take a party of schoolchildren on a trip overseas.

Your professional and career interests are likely to come to the fore this week. You seem to be enjoying a completely different setup and a new boss. New brooms sweep clean, they say, but in this case it can be a good thing. New ideas and ways of dealing with things can be good for you all around.

18th Week/April 30–May 6

Friday the 30th. Your group activities can include spiritual and charitable matters. Or you may be interested in film and photography. This can be a quite fascinating time for those of you who are involved in occult and psychic matters. You will feel really powerful and in control now. Creative activities and hobbies can include astrology or astronomy. Or some may prefer arts and crafts.

Saturday May 1st. Don't get too carried away when out at a dinner or on a date. You may tend to be uncharacteristically impulsive about spending a large sum of money. Your mood is likely to be both jolly and chatty. A relative can keep you amused with witty and lively conversation. You may learn a good deal about past family happenings. There may even be a scandal or two.

Sunday the 2nd. This is sure to be a very good time for those of you who want to get on with your own affairs. You can make the most of this day of rest. Those with spiritual inclinations may like to meditate, do yoga, or other spiritual disciplines. This is a good day for raising funds for charitable purposes. You may go visiting people in prison or the hospital. Bring them some spring flowers.

Monday the 3rd. The day will be delightful for those of you who like your own company or just being with your family. You may enjoy doing some research in archives and libraries. You will also enjoy entertaining at home. This can be a good time for dealing with decorating and other such activities. You seem to be in the mood to get things in order. You can put away the last of your winter gear.

Tuesday the 4th. You may enjoy a conversation with co-workers this morning. A meeting can also be fruitful. Some of you may consider it time to see a specialist about a person who is unwell. You can find it hard to relax, as you seem to have a lot of detailed things to sort through. The afternoon will be personally enjoyable, especially if meeting a friend. You may go out to dinner.

Wednesday the 5th. You will be relieved to hear that a creative project is going very well. You may be nearing the achievement of a certain goal you have set for yourself. This is a good day for getting on with hobbies and other interests in an organized fashion. Your self-discipline can really impress others. Those on a diet or exercise program will make far more progress than expected.

Thursday the 6th. It may be rather fun to speculate on a property matter. But you are wise to be cautious and uncommitted. Let others have the wild dreams that are probably so much hot air. You can find that a lover is making an impact on your feelings and ways of doing things. You should enjoy being with children. All personal and family matters, in fact, will be to your liking.

Weekly Summary

You can learn a lot from a group meeting or other event. In fact, teaming up with old friends after a short break can be cheerful and enjoyable. Some of you will be involved in group therapy or workshops of various kinds. These can certainly have an awakening effect on you and bring about a major change. However, they can be somewhat upsetting if preconceived ideas have to change too much.

Sunday can be a particularly good day for those of you who follow a spiritual path. Your receptiveness and sensitivity can be acute. A detached attitude toward life will help when dealing with those less fortunate and in need of help. You may spend some time dealing with relatives or simply helping those in homes, hospitals, or prisons. This can also be a favorable time to be on your own and more reflective.

Your personality tends to be a bit solemn and sober at the best of times. But this means that people know where they are with you and can rely upon you. You may achieve a position of some authority now and should use it to the best advantage.

19th Week/May 7–13

Friday the 7th. You can be a little troubled about some event that takes place at work early in the day. News of a personal kind can affect your job or family. A money matter may need sorting out in the afternoon. An official may be involved, or you may need to cut through a lot of red tape before you can claim what is due to you. You will need a great deal of patience.

Saturday the 8th. Your ability to resolve a financial problem can be helpful now. It may mean having to approach an individual who has power to help you. Or a parent may be able to bail you out at the last minute. This can be a really stressful day but good for working relations with others. Try to keep your temper with an unruly young person who may be going through a difficult phase.

Sunday the 9th. Those involved with the public can find things getting busy and lively now. You seem to be able to exercise a good deal of charm. If you are selling at a bazaar, having a meeting or rally, this can be useful. It can mean that everyone remains cheerful and in harmony. The day can be good for home entertaining too. You can be in the mood to cook dishes that delight all your guests.

Monday the 10th. This is likely to be a slow-moving but highly enjoyable day. You may tend to be a little quieter than usual and pretty noncommittal. Your efficiency and ability to get things organized can be useful at a local fair or other event. You may be glad to hear from an older brother or sister. Try to sound enthusiastic when chatting with a relative, even if you do not like the person.

Tuesday the 11th. A hobby such as stamp collecting is likely not to interest you now. You may feel a little let down by a youngster. Try not to be too disappointed when a lover fails to turn up at a meeting place. You probably will feel sort of worried and depressed, but this is likely to be a passing feeling. Life isn't always roses, and just now the thorns may be evident.

Wednesday the 12th. You can act in a caring enough fashion to a loved one but may not be all that sincere. It isn't always easy to please a moody mate or spouse. However, your attentiveness can help to change things in the end, so persevere. A family party can turn out well, but you may feel somewhat uninterested in it all. You are likely to keep to yourself and make excuses to no one.

Thursday the 13th. A change of atmosphere at home can occur quite unexpectedly. This may be due to a surprise visit from a friend. Or everyone will feel more expansive and cheerful just being together. However, your mood continues to be quite solemn and serious, especially at work. Life just isn't funny at present as far as you're concerned. So go about your business without inflicting your gloom on others.

Weekly Summary

The start of the week can see a minor panic over a money matter. It may simply be that someone wants to borrow a sum or arrange some special fees for business dealings with you. On the whole, you seem to be ready to help out, but be sure that all is dealt with sensibly and legally. A salary matter may need to be settled with your staff too. You have the feeling that someone is worth his or her weight in gold.

No one can call you the world's chattiest person at the best of times. But just now, your mind seems totally occupied with various thoughts about work or other serious matters. However, this can appear to relatives as moodiness or just plain boredom. So, maybe you need to explain that you do have a few things on your mind just now and aren't likely to be the life and soul of any gathering at present.

Family matters are likely to take over this week, and you can find yourself involved in parties, dinner dates, and various social events at home. Your enthusiasm may be markedly nil, but you are sure to do your best to be helpful all the same. You are more likely to enjoy a group event at home on Thursday.

20th Week/May 14–20

Friday the 14th. It isn't too easy to keep your mind on your hobbies or creative interests. You may keep dreaming about a lover. Try not to worry too much about a child's behavior. It's no good keeping him or her attached to your apron strings. You will feel a lot happier with a mate or spouse. You may deliberate about buying a certain item for the home. It may be too expensive.

Saturday the 15th. Impulse spending isn't really your way, but this day may see you suddenly make up your mind. You can decide that it is time to treat yourself to something new that you have wanted for a while. It may mean parting with a fairly large sum, which may bother you a bit. But in the long run you are sure to feel glad to have taken the plunge. You can enjoy admiring comments from others.

Sunday the 16th. Take things a little more easily, and stick to routine activities. You may feel a little overwrought or tired. It can be a good time for dealing with personal accounts and getting things in order. You may want to sort out files, old letters, or other bits and pieces that have accumulated. Those who are collecting for charities will be happy with the response now.

Monday the 17th. This can turn out to be a cheerful and happy-go-lucky day. You will feel that your relationship with others at work is improving daily. The day is especially good for those dealing with the public. Although you are likely to be kept busy, you can enjoy chats with people you meet. You may run into someone from the past or meet a lifelong friend. Spend time catching up on all the news.

Tuesday the 18th. Your mate or spouse may be in a quiet and calm mood at present. You can enjoy nature together in some way. Getting out into the countryside, being in pleasant parks and so on can be healing for your relationship. A lover will be delightful company just now for those uncommitted Capricorn people. You can feel happy in tested and tried relationships most of all.

Wednesday the 19th. A conversation with a partner is probably helpful. However, you may also feel a bit irritated by someone's lack of tact. Emotions can distort the truth of a situation. Maybe you need to dig a little deeper to get at the real facts. Legal matters are likely to be difficult to deal with. You may find that dealing with the public is hard work just now.

Thursday the 20th. Try not to cut corners or deal in dubious investments. You will be all too likely to lose a lot of joint cash that way. However, a private deal or investment may turn out best. You seem to be in a very cautious and anxious mood as far as any speculation or gambles are concerned. It will be wise not to take risks of any sort just now. Avoid the race track and the slot machines.

Weekly Summary

It can be a pretty trying time for those of you who are expecting or having children. Unexpected problems that arise can mean that you are kept in bed for a while. Those of you with older children may feel as if you are having to deal with all kinds of odd happenings and requests. However, a partner can be a real help in coping with youngsters this week.

Your workaday activities can be almost therapeutic at times. Putting your mind to life's little details and ordinary happenings may actually be soothing and distracting from any worries or problems. You still appear to be on pretty good terms with those you work with. You can offer your services to someone who may be unwell this week; this can be much appreciated, especially by an elderly person.

A mate or spouse is somewhat inclined to create waves this week. You may find yourself the target of someone's anger and annoyance. However, you don't need to lie down and take it all. Be sure to make your own views known also. Being together with a loved one in some beautiful place can help restore your balance and calm.

21st Week/May 21–27

Friday the 21st. This can be a time when all sorts of unexpected demands may be made on your time and money. However, you seem to be in a generous and expansive frame of mind and ready to oblige. A child or older student whom you are teaching may not find it easy to concentrate. You need to be patient and tolerant. The student may be having personal problems of which you are unaware.

Saturday the 22nd. This should turn out to be a good time for those of you who are studying or into research programs. You are likely to run up against a few problems with a very critical person at work. However, your ability to keep yourself and others well under control can come to the fore. People will find that your cool approach and practical methods work well so you will emerge with credit.

Sunday the 23rd. This is likely to be a favorable day for being with a mate or spouse. A legal matter, such as a separation or divorce, can be settled amicably now. You will really enjoy sharing your knowledge and understanding of a subject with a loved one. Your charm and protectiveness can warm someone's heart. Generally, this can turn out a peaceful and harmonious day.

Monday the 24th. You can find this a busy day for professional activities. The phone may keep ringing or you may be besieged by mail and paperwork. You can find that healing or counseling work is favored. In fact, you should be in a mood to give up your own needs to help others less fortunate or in pain. Communications with a special staff member can be extra good.

Tuesday the 25th. Some little reforms and changes at work can prove beneficial. You can enjoy a very useful conversation with one of your employees or a boss. The day is good for money matters too. It can be a time when cash seems to come your way as if by magic. You may find that a computer or a new car really helps you to deal with daily chores as well as professional requirements and needs.

Wednesday the 26th. It isn't always easy to keep calm at work, but if anyone can do it, you can. You may find that a partner or a member of the public is not acting in a cooperative manner at all. This, of course, will make you feel very irritable and moody. However, it isn't your way to let this flurry of dissension upset you or put you off what you have to do. Your course is set, and you will follow it.

Thursday the 27th. A group of people with whom you are dealing can prove quite disappointing. You may be let down by a most unreliable friend. A really special occasion you were planning may be canceled at the last minute. This can make you feel very depressed as well as annoyed. Your goals for the future can tend to be too idealistic or unrealistic just now. Wait for a more propitious time.

Weekly Summary

Students are likely to run up against a few problems when researching various details. You may find it hard to get down to the nitty-gritty of writing and routine work. Perhaps an older person can be of help. You can need some good advice on how to proceed with a very tricky subject or problem just encountered. Things will improve by Sunday, when you will feel more relaxed and can share your interests with a loved one.

Your career is likely to be one of the most important things in your life at present. Things are likely to be favorable for work-related matters this week. You can find that certain recent changes in administration or techniques you use can be beneficial to yourself and those you deal with. On the whole, you are likely to get on well with the public but may find people hard to work with on Wednesday.

Your social life may be disappointing this week. This in part can be due to your tiredness or lack of enthusiasm for your usual activities and interests. Perhaps it is time to take a little break from what has become boring and predictable. Try going to new places, seeing new faces.

22nd Week/May 28–June 3

Friday the 28th. Unexpected developments can stir things up a bit more than usual. You can find that a group activity is quite electric. A mate or spouse may arrange a surprise of some sort for you. You don't seem to be terribly happy about the arrangements though. If you insist on being critical and unkind, you can alienate a loved one. The day may be tiring but still quite rewarding.

Saturday the 29th. This should be a delightful time if spent quietly and privately with a loved one. You can feel more sensitive and yet compassionate toward others. This can get you involved in some sort of charitable or healing situation. You may have to care for someone who is not feeling well. The day is especially good for collecting and fund-raising of all kinds.

Sunday the 30th. A bit of an ego clash with a very judgmental person can occur. You may feel considerably upset if others are trying to pull your spirits down by being negative. This isn't likely to be a favorable time for entertaining at home. Things can go wrong in a major way. This might be because you feel irritable and lacking in humor this Memorial Day weekend.

Monday the 31st. If you feel up to it, you can achieve a lot professionally. This will be a far more cheerful day and your good humor restored. You can really enjoy being busy and keeping on the go if you are at work. You may run up against a powerful person who seems to have you just where he or she wants you. A loved one seems ready to try a new tack. A picnic can defuse any tensions.

Tuesday June 1st. This can turn out to be an ordinary, even dull, day. But you can make the most of any lull in activities by getting work planned and dealing with any private matters that have been put aside while you were busy. You may have to calm down a person who is not feeling well. But you are born to help others feel supported and steady, and this will be your chance to do so.

Wednesday the 2nd. Your calm and sensible approach can be helpful to a child. You may have to help the youngster deal with life's practicalities. A lover will be glad to see you after a long parting. You will be glad to spend time on quiet and serious hobbies and creative activities. A splendid classical performance at the theater can give you a lot to think about.

Thursday the 3rd. If you feel rushed off your feet by work, try to take some time to relax later in the day. You can find yourself getting just a bit irritated or over-wrought this morning. Later on you may feel a need to escape from everyone and everything. Your spiritual interests can seem a lot more important to you; you may attend an inspiring gathering.

Weekly Summary

Be prepared to put up with a period when you may be alone or left to your own devices by others. Your need to get away from it all and be peaceful can be fulfilled, but you may tend to regret it by Sunday. Those of you who are involved in healing matters, charitable occupations, and other self-sacrificing activities can do well now. Your ego doesn't seem to be a problem, but that of another person may well be.

Just quietly getting on with your duties and personal interests can keep you occupied. You may find this a somewhat quieter and more humdrum time than usual, but it seems to suit you well enough. You can feel that a partner is very supportive these days, and this makes you feel good. Your relationships and personal feelings can be very steady and practical right now.

You may find that the end of this week can be a time when you feel very detached about everything, especially money matters. This may surprise others who see you as a practical rather than a philanthropic person. But if you could just now, you would give it all to charity.

23rd Week/June 4–10

Friday the 4th. A thorough shake-up of all your finances may now be due. You may feel that you are beginning to run into debt again. This can be a good time to see a boss about a raise or loan. You may meet someone a bit unusual through your daily work. A meeting might help to get some staff problems worked out amicably. Everyone wants to end the week with a clean desk.

Saturday the 5th. This can be a very rewarding time for business matters. You may feel that you have worked hard and really earned what you have acquired. You will feel a lot happier now with your finances and can put some more money into an investment. A course you are taking to improve working facilities can be paying off. You will enjoy working with the media on behalf of your favorite organization.

Sunday the 6th. This can be a good time for making progress on hobbies and creative matters. But you may tend to get a bit too obsessed with something you consider highly important. It really can be time to lighten up and not take everything so seriously. Even your pleasures tend to be serious and heavy these days. Try to be less exacting. Time spent with young people can be cheerful.

Monday the 7th. A neighbor and you may fall out over some trivial matter. Take care not to be too critical of a brother or sister. You can find that someone who has recently joined you at work is really an exciting individual. You may want to be on more friendly terms with colleagues in general, but this one in particular will intrigue and challenge you.

Tuesday the 8th. Home matters have run a lot more smoothly of late. You become aware of a great deal of harmony and affection in your relationships with all your loved ones. It is a good time for joint money matters. A partner may want to discuss some large household item that is going to need purchasing. You are likely to be in a cooperative mood on this one and ready to make a sacrifice.

Wednesday the 9th. This may be a good time for some do-it-yourself work about the home. You can also feel like starting in on some changes to the garden. A group of friends may meet in your house to discuss a public event. The day is good for professional matters. It can still be a busy time for those at work, but you seem to have plenty of energy available.

Thursday the 10th. This can be a happy time for being with family and friends. You will feel ready to do a spot of home entertaining. Some of you may be planning to build an extension to your home. On the whole, dealings with property can be fortunate and work out as you plan. You will feel delighted to be in the company of a lover this afternoon and may linger into the evening.

Weekly Summary

You need to take an overview of your personal financial situation now, especially if a lot has been spent on children's education or other necessities. On the whole, you are likely to feel that all is going well and that there are no major problems. This may give you scope to consider a new car, computer, or some other electronic gadget. These may all be helpful for business purposes and can be considered necessary expenses.

This will be an important time for those involved in studies and teaching activities. You can be trying hard to get some research and private study straightened out. Exams may be looming ahead, but you may not yet feel ready for them. You may be really busy with various jobs and errands this week that can keep you running around the local neighborhood.

People you knew in the past may now turn up again in your life. This can be a pleasant experience on the whole, and you can have a lot to discuss, old photos to look over, and reminiscences to share. For some of you, these reunions may be from military times together. Property dealings can do well now, although you seem to be a trifle worried about a repair bill.

24th Week/June 11–17

Friday the 11th. This seems to be a somewhat trying time. You may find it hard to relax and just enjoy yourself. Why take things so seriously all the time? A dutiful attitude toward a child is fine but not loving. Perhaps you are feeling too tired and dispirited to go ahead with a hobby or creative interest. Try to relax a little and unwind. Try to do the absolute minimum.

Saturday the 12th. You will feel better if you can see a doctor as soon as possible. Your nerves may have been stretched a lot of late. Your sympathy for a fellow worker will be gratefully received. A pet can give you a whole lot of pleasure and healing. While it is a favorable day for those buying clothing and food for business purposes, you may actually be more interested in medical matters.

Sunday the 13th. Alternative medicines and therapies can do you a lot of good. You may decide that a visit to an acupuncturist is what you need most. Making a fresh start in some activity connected with your job can lead to greater things. A new person may join your firm or office. This can cause a little ripple of excitement and interest in the routine activities.

Monday the 14th. This can be a very happy and cheerful time just for dealing with everyday matters. You will laugh and joke with staff and colleagues and feel most good-humored. A tax refund, inheritance, or other nice little windfall can help a lot to make you even happier. Get on with all sorts of jobs that need to be dealt with, such as clearing out old clothes or paying bills.

Tuesday the 15th. A steady and reliable relationship is what you like best. You can enjoy the company of a serious, perhaps elderly, person, whose wisdom and philosophical approach to life is just what you like to hear about. You will be more than glad to see a long-time lover again after a fairly long separation. In dealings with children, you can provide help and understanding.

Wednesday the 16th. You may find that the morning is a difficult time for dealings with a mate or spouse. You may have to put up with someone's extreme annoyance about something. A lack of humor may make you both take matters far too seriously. Try to remain as tactful and courteous as you can. But it seems that someone is pushing you just a little bit too far, and you will have to draw a line.

Thursday the 17th. A boss or other authority figure seems ready to come to terms over a proposed pay raise. You may need to cut off children's pocket money if they are behaving badly. This can be a day when financial matters seem frustrating and difficult to deal with. Officials and red tape may not help where a business matter is concerned, so you may have to make an end run around them.

Weekly Summary

You may now feel a bit depressed about the outcome of some creative project you have embarked on. It can be hard to keep going when inspiration appears to have run out. But don't let that worry you too much. Even Michelangelo felt like this at times. Try to be disciplined, and tackle a hobby or creative venture a little at a time.

You should be feeling a lot better in regard to your

health these days. Some healing or special treatment
may have cost a lot. But it is sure to be worth it when
you realize how fit you now feel. Hospital treatment
may have been necessary for some of you Capricorn
people. If you work in the field of medicine, this is
likely to be a good week for seeing good results in your
work. You can feel very caring and compassionate toward those who need help this way.

Maybe you are beginning to realize just how reliable
and supportive your mate or spouse can be. You can
get into some philosophical discussions together about
family matters or the past. But neither of you lacks
practicality or the realistic approach.

25th Week/June 18–24

Friday the 18th. A swift decision on a money matter
can save you a good deal. You should feel ready to
expand in a business and professional sense. This is a
good day for all dealings with the public. Your cheerful
and lively manner certainly will go over well with people at work as well. You will get a lot done now that
you are feeling so much more energetic.

Saturday the 19th. You may take someone's cool and
distant attitude to heart. Or you yourself may act this
way toward another. All in all, the message seems to
be that a love affair is coming to an end or going
through a very sticky patch. It may be wise to separate
for a while. It's a truism that absence often makes the
heart grow fonder, as you are likely to realize now.

Sunday the 20th. Discussing a vacation with your partner can be very pleasant, but you may not find it very
easy to agree where you want to go. However, your
mood is liberal and generous at present, so you are
more likely to be prepared to compromise. An air of
confidence and cheerfulness can show others just how

much your health and spirits have improved over recent weeks.

Monday the 21st. This can be a very favorable time for you professionally. You may see a dream come true in some way. A humanitarian and caring attitude toward others means that your business is likely to flourish. Some of you may have to take on more private work these days to make ends meet. You may be involved in some aspect of psychology or healing work. Do not be afraid to make decisions.

Tuesday the 22nd. Relationships with others at work and with the public in general seem harmonious and delightful just now. Make the most of it, as these things tend to come and go. You may find that an unexpected bonus from a boss or client is coming to you now. You are likely to find it hard to put your feelings into words when talking to your partner, but he or she will surely understand.

Wednesday the 23rd. Try not to overdo things and dissipate all your newfound energy. The morning may be particularly hectic. This can be a day when you tend to feel everything very intensely and deeply. A special friend can have some sudden news to tell you that may give you a bit of a shock. An investment may do badly just now and you may consider selling out.

Thursday the 24th. You may feel quite troubled about a friend or a group of people with whom you are involved. You are likely to be a little sad and out of sorts. Some of your worries may be due to a money matter that you haven't yet been able to straighten out. At times you will really feel as if all your hopes have been dashed. But take heart and keep going. Remember the adage about the light at the end of the tunnel.

Weekly Summary

If you decide to go away this weekend, you may regret the whole idea. You just don't seem to be in a mood for enjoying and relaxing. You tend to be far too busy worrying about money matters and other problems just now. So maybe you would be wiser to save your money and plan something for the future instead. You will find in-laws boring and uncommunicative these days.

Whatever else is happening in your life just now, you seem to be doing well professionally at least. This is thanks to the fact that you are really giving of yourself and your time to help those less fortunate or needy. Many of you may be involved in medical matters or healing others in some way. This can be a week when you will see some real results in this direction. It is likely to be a harmonious time for dealing with bosses.

You need to brace yourself for some fairly difficult news or reactions from a friend. Their own private life can spill over into yours. However, it may be hard to know just how to help someone in trouble. It can be a time for standing by people you love and giving them support and strength.

26th Week/June 25–July 1

Friday the 25th. Take some time to discuss things with a friend or partner. It can help someone to have a good listener. You will enjoy a group meeting tonight. You may have a good deal more to say than usual. However, this is also a time for letting others know how you feel about a very emotional issue. You may start making some decisions about your career and personal future now.

Saturday the 26th. Your desire for peace and quiet may lead you to go on a retreat. You really do seem to need to get away from it all. For some of you, this can be quite a special and spiritual time. You can reevaluate your life on less materialistic terms. You may find that a partner is in the mood to talk and talk. But you do not have to listen to every word.

Sunday the 27th. Unexpected matters can arise concerning a will or an insurance policy. You can really enjoy the company of a special and much valued friend. Just being alone with a loved one can be very revitalizing and pleasant. You may learn that a financial investment has taken a turn for the better. Naturally this can cheer you up a good deal. And it can turn a dull day bright.

Monday the 28th. Although a good deal of work may be piling up, you now seem to be better able to relax and take it all on board. The morning can be a good time for those working out of their homes. You should get a good deal done in peace and quiet. Later, you may have some sort of conflict with a partner or legal representative. But stand up for your rights, whatever may be said by others.

Tuesday the 29th. This is likely to be a good time for straightening out any personal matters. You will be in the mood to enjoy yourself in your own quiet and serious way. This may mean arranging to be alone to enjoy some serious reading or writing. Or you can go with a lover to see a good play or musical concert. Children can act very responsibly now, giving you a preview of their future.

Wednesday the 30th. Maybe you will get a bit irate with someone this morning. There are times when even your diplomacy fails to help. You may really have to lay down the law on a certain matter. You are likely to find that your evening is expensive. You may think you can woo a lover by being extravagant. But it doesn't seem to be working at all, so you have to rethink your strategies.

Thursday July 1st. A letter or a phone call you receive can make you feel a bit worried. It may concern some financial deal or other money matter. You will have to work hard to get things under control again. In fact, it may be necessary to raise a private loan from somewhere. A child can prove something of a problem as well. You may need the advice of someone older and wiser.

Weekly Summary

You probably will keep a pretty low profile at the start of the week. A good many little private matters may have to be seen to and cleared up. Drawing up wills, sorting out health insurance, or getting things organized for retirement can take up time. Your need at present is to tie up as many loose ends as you can before setting off on a new phase.

You may be totally absorbed in your own interests and activities just now. Others may feel that you are being selfish or unapproachable. This can cause a bit of a rift on Monday when the Full Moon creates its usual tensions. You are likely to take a cool, serious, and very practical approach to all you do. Your career may seem to be the most important thing in your life and all that can fulfill you personally just now. This is hardly flattering to a partner.

Some very upsetting money matter can come up at the end of this period. You may feel you have all the bad luck in the world at times. But it may be that your negative or overly cautious attitude is at the bottom of some of your problems.

27th Week/July 2–8

Friday the 2nd. You are likely to go in for a little impulse buying this holiday weekend. This may be because you want to impress a lover by going to the best places, wearing the best things. Try not to make too many waves with a loved one. Someone you relied on may want to get out of a financial arrangement. This will put you out considerably and have an unfortunate effect on your plans for the future.

Saturday the 3rd. Make a definite decision this morning, and don't shilly-shally about. It can be important to remain detached and tactful when dealing with an accountant. The afternoon will be a good time for pleasurable activities. You can enjoy watching a thriller at the theater, or you can have a good time at a local sports match. Your team has a good chance of winning.

Sunday the 4th. This holiday can be a very good time for teachers and those connected with children's education. A certain child can make you feel very proud if you are a parent or teacher. It can be a real morale booster when you see good results for your years of hard work when meeting former students at some patriotic event or concert. A certain individual in your neighborhood can help out in a practical way with some problem.

Monday the 5th. Be prepared to get going on a good many tasks about the house and yard. You can find this a good day for any dealings or investments in real estate. In fact, for some of you this can be a time to find your dream house. Being sympathetic and attentive toward a parent or other family member can be your good deed for the day. Patience will be necessary and rewarding.

Tuesday the 6th. Plans and agreements may need careful scrutiny. You can find this a good time to sign any documents relating to property matters. You may find that a partner is not altogether happy about some arrangement. Try to listen to the point of view of that person before going ahead. You may get around to writing or phoning close relatives and may have some good news to tell them.

Wednesday the 7th. This is likely to be a harmonious and relaxed morning at home or spent with the family. However, things may get a lot more hectic and out of control by the afternoon. You will feel a bit restless by then and may want to do something energetic or practical. Take the children swimming or to some sports event. You may take in a good movie later on.

Thursday the 8th. It isn't always easy to get through to a youngster on an educational matter. You may tend to take too authoritarian and stern an attitude. This is likely to cause a bit of a rebellious reaction. You may find it hard to relax and just enjoy yourself. You have to watch that tendency to take life a good deal too seriously. You will find life a lot easier if you lighten up.

Weekly Summary

You may be faced with a do-or-die situation this week. It may be necessary to cut your losses in some areas and give up on a particular business deal. However, this is likely to work to your advantage in the long run. You can earn quite a bit from overtime, but take care not to wear yourself out in the process.

This is a favorable time for those of you who are working with local sports teams or theatricals. Those of you who are busy with bazaars, children's parties, or church matters will feel expansive and cheerful. You are likely to have a good time. A foreign neighbor may invite you over for a get-together. This can broaden your outlook considerably and add to local goodwill. You may find a neighbor most helpful and supportive just when you need it.

Something from the past can come up this week. A mystery or family secret may be solved. You will be on very good terms with the family these days. This is due in large part to a more caring and compassionate attitude rather than your usual cool and aloof one. Giving out love means that you are likely to get it back as well.

28th Week/July 9–15

Friday the 9th. This can turn out to be a costly day if you aren't careful. It is not a good time to speculate or gamble. The morning may see you having a lover's quarrel. Try not to be quite so dramatic about everything. Later in the day, you are likely to feel more sympathetic about another's point of view. You may have to take care of a person who is sick, which can cause a change in your plans.

Saturday the 10th. Visiting a sick person or taking someone to a hospital can take up a good part of the day. You may have to deal with pets who are showing worrisome symptoms. You can find that a meeting about business and joint finances can produce some innovative new ideas. However, your present mood is not optimistic, and you may not want to go along with any proposals.

Sunday the 11th. This is likely to be a far more relaxed morning. You can get going on various little accounting jobs and other daily activities. If you have been sick, you will feel a lot more rested now. The afternoon seems to turn out very promising, especially when a partner shows you love and affection. It can make you feel protected and nurtured.

Monday the 12th. This can be an organized and disciplined day. It is sure to make you feel good, as you like to have things under control. You can enjoy yourself following serious and interesting pursuits. Some of you may enjoy practical activities such as gardening or woodwork. A partner can be very supportive just now. You will find yourself much encouraged.

Tuesday the 13th. This should be a good time to make a new start in a partnership of any kind. In fact, for some it may be a time to get engaged or married. The morning is a particularly auspicious time for such events. Later in the day, you may find that you have mismanaged some money matter and have spent a good deal more than you meant to. It is time for some review of your budget.

Wednesday the 14th. Some private investment or work can help to restore your finances again. However, you may have to cancel some arrangement or date in order to work overtime. You can feel a bit upset about this but deem it necessary. This day is better for dealings with younger people than with older ones. An official may be quite annoying, but you will feel powerless to do anything.

Thursday the 15th. This is likely to be a pleasant day when you can make some plans for a vacation. Capricorn students and teachers should get some time now to relax after hard work in summer classes and study for exams. Now you can put your books away and plan some other interests just for yourself. On the whole, this can turn out to be a fairly quiet day with little happening of note.

Weekly Summary

You seem to be involved with either your own health problems or those of another. It can be a time for making dental appointments, seeing to routine health checks, and so on. You may be considering starting on some sort of strict health regimen now in order to purify yourself. However, don't overdo it. You tend to be a little hard on yourself at times. You can let up a bit on Sunday morning and sleep later or have a giant breakfast.

A partnership can be very special just now. If it is a

business one, you can feel that you are being well supported. It is likely that any practical arrangements are working out well between you now. Some of you may be seeing to the last details of your marriage plans. You will feel serious but also quietly happy about your love life.

Those of you who are involved in business matters still have a lot to work out in this area. You may have to reorganize certain investments, joint financial matters, taxes, and so on. Having an official breathing down your neck can be very constraining at times.

29th Week/July 16–22

Friday the 16th. For those on vacation this should be a very favorable day. You can find a long journey most enjoyable, especially if you pass by beautiful scenery. The day also is good for any musical, artistic, or theatrical productions. You are quite likely to be involved in managing such events. Your attitude toward life is likely to be highly pragmatic at the present.

Saturday the 17th. Taking a steady approach to something you are studying seems the best way. You can be interested in serious or classical subjects just now. Research and interest in scholarly matters may motivate you now, especially if you are writing or lecturing. A journey should go as planned and on time. You will act dutifully toward an in-law who comes for a visit.

Sunday the 18th. Those of you who are involved in church work or some other spiritual path will now feel deeply about it all. You may be inclined to help out with charitable pursuits as well. Plans for rebuilding or buying property for a place of worship can now be discussed more carefully. You will feel very loving and will enjoy the company of children. An afternoon at the beach will be pleasant.

Monday the 19th. You will find that a new job is a good deal more stimulating than the old. You may have to discuss some very private financial matters with a relative. Some of you may be drawing up a will or other important document. It is a good time for all money matters. Be ready to jump in and don't hang back. This can be a good time for signing agreements and making sales.

Tuesday the 20th. A boss can make life trying this morning. You may fall out with a mate or spouse over something trivial. Your optimism seems to disappear this afternoon, and you may be disillusioned by someone. A friend appears to be unreliable just now, and this may upset you more than you expect. It may just be that you are feeling tired and oversensitive.

Wednesday the 21st. This is likely to be an argumentative time for a talk or group meeting. You can be a bit timid about putting over your point of view. However, try not to be too serious about it all, and keep a sense of humor. Some revolutionary new ideas for making extra cash can upset your sense of security. Try to be less fearful of the future while exercising caution in the present.

Thursday the 22nd. A group of friends may decide to have a quiet evening together. You can enjoy an outing or a date with a friend whose company relaxes you. The day is good for making progress on various hobbies and practical interests. On the whole, this can be a humdrum or fairly routine kind of day. But this may suit your calm and quiet temperament best of all.

Weekly Summary

This can be a good week for those of you who are going on vacations. You will be looking forward to a little peace and quiet in the countryside or in some beauty spot. Many of you are likely to try and incorporate a little culture or scholarliness in your trip. This can be interesting and can also help expand the mind to include new and fresh ideas. It will also be a good week for those involved in studies of various kinds.

You may have a good deal more involvement with the public than usual over the weekend. This may be connected with church activities or other spiritual interests. Changes in your professional life can be unsettling just now. But it may be necessary to hear a boss out before starting to worry; you probably are too negative or critical in your judgments or opinions due to your innate sense of caution.

This can be a pretty mixed time for social interests. Some group activities can still keep you busy. You may tend to feel a great need to escape or get away from certain group obligations that still hold you. A friend seems to be acting oddly or unreliably. This may lead to disagreements.

30th Week/July 23–29

Friday the 23rd. Now it may be a good deal easier to get along with a special friend or partner. You may still be very intense about your feelings, but it can be easier just to be yourself with another. The latter part of the day is likely to be spent in private. You may feel like listening to some pleasant music and relaxing alone. Getting to bed early can be beneficial.

Saturday the 24th. You can decide to make some important changes in your personal finances. A group of people that you belong to may meet privately or secretly. You will enjoy being with a particular friend, discussing philosophy or astrology. The day is good for any spiritual activities. New medical advances can benefit your health now. Ask your doctor about such treatments.

Sunday the 25th. This can be a fortunate and happy day for you. You are inclined to be alone, but being away from crowds should feel very good at present. Religious matters can flourish; your understanding of such matters can increase. In fact, you may be inclined to read books with a philosophical or religious content. Legal writings or travel books can also absorb you just now.

Monday the 26th. You can be quite bowled over by an attractive foreign person. A long-time lover can be good company tonight. You may find that an older child can relate to you far more. In fact, you can feel that you are real friends now. A risky undertaking may need reviewing. You are not likely to be in a position at the present moment to take a gamble financially.

Tuesday the 27th. This can tend to be a quite confusing day. You may feel obliged to hide certain facts about your finances. An auditor or bank manager may ask to see you about joint accounts and other business matters. Perhaps you have been overoptimistic or have spent too much of late. A child is likely to be a bit dramatic and silly, but console yourself with the thought that it is only a phase.

Wednesday the 28th. Your thoughts may tend to circulate around financial problems. You may be wondering just how to straighten out some kind of muddle you appear to be in. It may be necessary to consult an expert on the subject. This can be a time when a detached attitude is best. Board and staff meetings can take up time and energy and may not resolve anything, to your disappointment.

Thursday the 29th. You may find that unexpected news about a money matter adds to your gloom. But try to keep yourself from being too negative or self-critical. You may begin to feel that you have failed in some way. A child can annoy you with a sudden request for financial help when you have little enough to spare. Try to be reasonable and talk it through. You may find a new source of income.

Weekly Summary

The start of this week can be pleasant, especially if you have some time in which to reflect, meditate, or just read and enjoy private pursuits of your own. You may find it a good time to finish up various outstanding matters so that you can be ready for any new ventures that come up. It can also be a time for a renewal of good health and fitness. Alternative treatments may interest you greatly just now.

You can be at your most calm, charming, and gentle over the weekend. This seems to be an attractive mixture for those who love you. You may try to take on a great deal and make too many plans for the future. Although your personal activities tend to be low-key, others may be urging you to try to be a little more adventurous and take a few risks in life.

This seems to be a trying time for financial matters. You may be obliged to see an accountant, bank manager, or some other individual who seems to have a lot of influence, What that person has to say doesn't appear to be too cheering. It may be that you have expected too much from a recent investment. It may not be your fault, so don't blame yourself too much.

31st Week/July 31–August 5

Friday the 30th. A trip or long journey you undertake can be very enjoyable. You can feel happy when with a loved one. Try not to overdo the charm when dealing with an instructor or a foreigner. It can turn out to be a busy day with lots of comings and goings in your local area. Neighbors may drop in for a chat or ask you to drop around for an evening of conversation or watching television.

Saturday the 31st. Your intense attitude toward a local situation may stir up some reactions from others. However, you seem to be able to stir up people's consciences about matters concerning handicapped children, local homes for old people, and so on. You may be able to get the support of a powerful and influential individual, although little can be accomplished over this weekend.

Sunday August 1st. This can turn out to be a positive morning for discussions and meetings. A brother or sister may have some important news for you. You can be busier than usual with neighbors, or close relatives may get in touch. You can feel sympathetic toward a family member who may ask for help. Dealings with property can look promising this coming week.

Monday the 2nd. Any repairs or alterations to your home and surroundings can be successfully dealt with now. Your dealings with a fairly important individual can mean a change in finances. You may be asked to take over administration of some exciting business venture. Generally this will be a much more stimulating and interesting day than you have had in a while.

Tuesday the 3rd. You can find that communications with a partner are not a bit straightforward. This may be because you are letting emotional matters interfere with clear thinking. Try not to get too irate or bring up all kinds of past annoyances. It would be best to postpone signing a document for the time being. You don't really seem that clear about what you want.

Wednesday the 4th. You may be a little disappointed in a film or theater show. A lover seems to have let you down lately. Maybe you are beginning to see things more realistically and less romantically now. On the whole, you seem calm and thoughtful about life. Money matters still seem to be worrying you. Listen carefully to the advice of someone in the know.

Thursday the 5th. This can turn out to be a far more satisfying day than yesterday. You should be a lot better organized and able to see some results of your efforts. A recent decision taken with a partner can now work to your advantage. You can have a very happy time with a lover. Children can also be good fun, and you may be able to take them on a pleasant trip to the shore or an amusement park.

Weekly Summary

Some of you Capricorn people are likely to be involved in various local organizations or societies. This sort of thing is usually right up your alley, as you enjoy running things in your own quiet and efficient manner. On the whole, such local interests and politics can be favorable this week. You may be in the right places and seem to be in touch with all the right people. Make use of these contacts to help your campaigns.

Home concerns can take over during the week, and you may have many plans afoot. This can be a good time for repairs, expanding to make more room, or decorating the home as you would like it. Older Capricorns may now get out in the garden and relax or putter about. It is likely to be a lively time with plenty of activity and family events to celebrate. You can catch up on the gossip when relatives call or write.

It will be time now for a little quiet enjoyment in your own practical and peaceful Capricorn way. Although at times you can feel somewhat dissatisfied or even disinterested in anything but serious matters, you seem better able to let go and have some fun this week.

32nd Week/August 6–12

Friday the 6th. You may be a bit impractical about a money matter now. Collecting for charity should go well. Your daily activities may involve healing work or dealing with small animals. It will not be an easy time for travelers, although a plane journey can be exciting. However, a seaside vacation can be delightful and help you to relax again. You are likely to make new friends.

Saturday the 7th. Unusual people you meet can make this an exciting day. You may be asked to go in to work unexpectedly. An invitation to go out may be expensive, but you may not like to refuse. Keep an eye out for a swift change of events in a business situation. A quite difficult interview may take place with a certain rebellious individual. There may be no definite outcome.

Sunday the 8th. This weekend you will feel very happy and relaxed with a mate or spouse. Relations with others are sure to be helped by a lot of tact and charm. You will be a lot more tolerant than usual, especially with children. A vacation in some lovely place may now be working wonders for you and a partner. Theatrical performances can be most enjoyable. You can choose something suitable for youngsters.

Monday the 9th. It isn't always easy to keep calm when children are being naughty. You may tend to play the heavy hand with youngsters just now. At times you may feel as if little can go right. A mate or spouse may try to cheer you up by taking you out tonight. But you are likely to prove pretty gloomy company. To change your mood, look at the ads and plans a shopping spree tomorrow.

Tuesday the 10th. A conversation with a partner can prove helpful this morning. You may find this a good time for putting across your ideas in a lecture or by letter. It may seem hard to make a definite decision about a money matter later in the day. You are likely to find it a good time for buying stocks or getting bargains at the sales. A new item of clothing can be exciting.

Wednesday the 11th. You need to be abreast of what is going on in the financial world. Joint business partnerships and family accounts need to be looked at with care. You may enjoy spending on a special occasion of some kind tonight. A group of people can make you feel unwanted. This can be upsetting, but you will manage to hold your temper in the face of provocation.

Thursday the 12th. You can have a very happy day away from it all. A trip to an art gallery or some lovely scenic place can lift your spirits again. You are likely to be more philosophical just now. But some secret problem still seems to be nagging away in the background. You will enjoy a meeting with a lover. Legal matters can go well; a long negotiation can come to an end.

Weekly Summary

Daily activities at work are likely to include accounting and other money matters. This can mean giving out bonuses or pay raises to staff or colleagues. You may be ready to make a few changes now in your usual routines; even a steady person like yourself may now feel a desire to have a bit of variety in the humdrum activities of everyday life. Even a change of route to work can mean seeing fresh sights.

Your mate or spouse will be in a happy and cheerful mood this weekend, and this kind of feeling tends to be infectious. Sunday can be a very enjoyable day for you and loved ones. If you are dealing with legal matters this week, you are likely to find that a settlement is greatly to your advantage. This promises to be a pleasant time for relationships with others.

Your desire to improve joint finances may lead you to try new or unorthodox methods of raising capital. However, you will be wise to take things cautiously and not listen to all the enthusiastic talk that others give you. They may just be eager to make a fast buck at your expense. Take special care on Wednesday when frustrating events or sudden tax demands can really set you back.

33rd Week/August 13–19

Friday the 13th. Despite the inauspicious date, all should go well. You can quietly enjoy a vacation break or an outing with a group of special friends. Older people can be better company than you expected. You may have to take a group of children on an outing or bus tour, but all should proceed smoothly enough if you organize things well in advance.

Saturday the 14th. A professional matter can cause you some indecision. In the end, however, you may find that you feel sorry for someone in need. This can be the ruling factor if you are involved in one of the healing professions. You need to take great care when signing documents or making agreements. Don't be too trusting of others, however smooth-talking they may seem. They can take advantage of you.

Sunday the 15th. Your public image seems to be very favorable just now. This can help greatly when it comes to professional matters. You may feel a need to change or reform certain aspects of your working life. You can start to implement some changes this weekend. In fact, some of you may consider taking on an entirely new job and breaking free from past restrictions.

Monday the 16th. Your charm can win the day when trying to explain a financial matter. In fact, this can be a good time for those dealing with the public, especially in a selling capacity. A desire to beautify your workaday environment may lead to spending some cash on new furnishings. Try not to be careless when dealing with an agreement or going through important files.

Tuesday the 17th. You may be somewhat disillusioned by a friend's attitude. Although you may feel very angry about something, it may have to be kept under a lid. You could suspect that a talk you give to a group of people is not going over too well. Try to make the best of a very dreary social occasion tonight. It may be important to be there for business purposes or to maintain a high profile.

Wednesday the 18th. You really don't seem to be enjoying anything much at present. Even a surprise or unexpected outing fails to relieve your gloom. This may be because you have been overdoing things of late and not having any fun. All work and no play makes Jack a dull boy, they say, and the same applies to Jill. So cancel an engagement and have a rest. Don't feel duty-bound to go along.

Thursday the 19th. You are likely to upset someone you meet early in the day by being a bit tactless. The morning can be a quite difficult time for a social occasion. A real desire to get away from it all can take you off to somewhere private and peaceful this afternoon. You may enjoy a good film or video. A book you read now can have a profound effect on you.

Weekly Summary

Your professional life seems to be undergoing a few changes of late. This may be needed if you are to keep up with current trends and ideas. New ways of attracting customers or improving the look of your workplace can all help to make a new image for your business. You seem to be enjoying more relaxed and pleasant relationships with staff and colleagues now. Naturally this makes work a happier place for everyone.

You just aren't in the mood for much socializing this week. You may be feeling a little tired from working too hard or simply not inclined to make small talk. This might cause you to cancel various engagements or put off friends. All this may not always be well received by others, but you will be wise to take a break and have a rest. Don't drag yourself to events out of a sense of misplaced duty or martyrdom.

Your need to be on your own may mean spending some time in your study. You can be in the mood to contemplate, meditate, do your yoga exercise, or simply sit back with a good video or book. This can often lead to some quite profound ideas and plans for the future.

34th Week/August 20–26

Friday the 20th. A letter can bring some good news about a business matter. Just working away quietly behind the scenes can please you. You Capricorn people seldom try to seek the limelight. Dealings with a bank manager or other important individuals will be quite successful. You can be on good terms with the kind of people who can help you financially.

Saturday the 21st. This is likely to be a very pleasant and happy day. You may feel as if money worries are a thing of the past. You are likely to feel centered and confident about your own abilities. Artistic matters or a musical show can liven up the evening. Spiritual interests may be paramount for some Capricorn people. Your health is sure to benefit from the general sense of calm and peace.

Sunday the 22nd. Personal plans seem to be working well and to your advantage now. Your air of calm confidence can help others to feel happy and relaxed in your company. Children will give a lot of pleasure. You also are likely to be in a creative mood and may enjoy working on your favorite hobbies. Getting out in the garden or countryside can make you feel on top of the world.

Monday the 23rd. An organized approach to your life means some ambitions can now be fulfilled or can at least get under way. You seem to be able to channel your energies a lot better just now. A money matter tends to turn into a spot of bother and may need some quick thinking to straighten out. Unexpected tax bills or insurance premium payments can come as a bit of a shock.

Tuesday the 24th. A subtle approach to a financial situation may be best. But try not to entertain too many hopes about a certain deal or speculative venture. You need to take a more thorough and practical approach toward a creative matter. A pleasant evening out will go a long way toward restoring your spirits. You are likely to feel irritable about a child's behavior.

Wednesday the 25th. Things can be transformed quite rapidly if you let them flow at their own pace. However, you tend to hold back too much or act too defensively. Try not to take such a negative view of your financial and business situation. You may get depressed about a child's difficult or careless behavior. A serious talk may give you clues to the problem.

Thursday the 26th. If you can keep your temper this morning, you may be able to steer around a very tricky situation. A particular friend may be causing trouble behind your back. You need to be very careful about a certain financial investment. It doesn't look as though a boss or other influential figure is prepared to help you or bail you out if the investment turns sour.

Weekly Summary

Your week will begin quite happily and lightly. You are most likely to be busy working away at things that interest you but that require little limelight or fanfare. Those of you who are involved in charitable or religious work can just keep on helping others without fuss. This can be a time for hospital or prison visiting or caring for old folks in a nursing home. Others may want to find peace of mind on a retreat.

You will be feeling more confident and a good deal more lighthearted during the weekend. Those of you with religious inclinations can gain a lot of peace and happiness from going to church, mosque, or synagogue. Generally, this can be a good period for dealing with any personal ambitions and desires. You can spread more happiness than you realize when in such a contented mood. Others will look to you for support and steadiness, knowing they can rely on your word.

Take care when trying to deal with a certain financial situation after the weekend. You may now tend to draw back when it is really time to move forward. Try to use your instincts more so that you will know just when to make the right moves.

35th Week/August 27–September 2

Friday the 27th. Your bold and practical approach to a local situation can work wonders. A neighbor may help you out with the children. This is a good time for shopping and traveling around your local area. This can be quite a busy time for you with lots of phone calls, letters, and other interesting communications. A relative may ask you around for dinner. Do not turn down the invitation.

Saturday the 28th. This can turn out to be a very good day for those involved in writing and teaching. You will be delighted to get the results of a recent little gamble or speculative venture. A meeting with an instructor or student should be very enjoyable. You may feel that you are making good progress now with any studies or reading that you have been pursing lately.

Sunday the 29th. You will be a lot more peaceful now when you are at home. In fact, at present it can seem the ideal place to be. You may find that this is a good time to get started on some home repairs that have long been pending. Your best bet will be to try to use this time to investigate as many financial matters or pay as many bills as you can. Then you will know exactly where you stand.

Monday the 30th. This is likely to prove to be a very relaxed and quiet day and one to be spent with the family. On the whole, things tend to be harmonious between you and loved ones. However, certain topics of conversation do seem to stir up a lot of feeling. It may be best to steer clear of these if there is any chance of their causing rifts. A brother or sister can be quite irritating.

Tuesday the 31st. Plans and ideas about how to redecorate the home or build an extension to it can occupy your conversation early in the day. You may also discuss money matters with a parent. If you do get together with a relative, this can be a time for remembering the past together. You can meet a foreign person and take an instant dislike to the individual.

Wednesday September 1st. You may feel a bit uncomfortable with a lover. In fact, a sudden separation can occur. Naturally this can be upsetting and depressing. However, all need not be lost. Just the same, you will need time to try to discover what is at the root of your mutual problems. A child can be hard to control or just rebellious.

Thursday the 2nd. Try to express bluntly what you are feeling. Bottling things up will only make you ill and unhappy. You may feel it is time to deal with a child more severely. The afternoon can be the best time for workaday matters. In fact, just getting ahead with life's usual little details should be soothing and healing. A message from overseas may go astray, causing some confusion.

Weekly Summary

The start to the week is likely to be busy with lots of comings and goings. There are times like this when you may wish the phone had never been invented. Try to deal with as much correspondence and paperwork as you can. You may need to catch up on all the calls you have been meaning to make. This can clear your mind and help to get things more in perspective.

It will be a good time to be at home if you can have a little break. Then you can enjoy meeting relatives who may be visiting and discussing old times together. A party at home or a dinner for you and your friends will be successful and interesting. You can enjoy discussing some deep topics and solving the problems of the world together. It will be a good time for those who enjoy do-it-yourself work and want to do a spot of home decorating.

The week seems to end on a somewhat sour note. You may be having a lot more to do with children, especially as you get them ready to return to school. Clothes, books, and other matters may need to be seen to. If youngsters tend to be moody and rebellious, this just adds to your own sense of irritation and annoyance.

36th Week/September 3–9

Friday the 3rd. It can come as a pleasant surprise to find that you have a refund, bonus, or other monetary gain. You may be in the mood to make a gift to a loved one to show how special he or she is to you. A little trip to hear some interesting lecture or attend a conference or meeting can make the day more varied. In fact, some of you may be starting a new course of studies now.

Saturday the 4th. It isn't always easy to show others that you care. But now you can get a chance to show a partner your feelings in practical and positive ways.

You may have to keep a certain little trip or piece of news secret for a while in order to spring a surprise. Youngsters can be a source of amusement and fun, especially if they are engaged in theatricals.

Sunday the 5th. Your partner is sure to show you just how dependable he or she can be. You may have a lot of work to do in private and can take yourself off to your study. This should be a good day for organizing yourself and your interests so that a lot is done in a short space of time. You can enjoy classical music or the theater with a lover. Or you may prefer a romantic dinner at home.

Monday the 6th. Try to keep things simple this holiday. You can end up getting in a muddle if you try to deal with too many financial or other matters. You may regret having been involved in some dubious speculative ventures. Or you may wonder now just why you trusted someone who has been proved unreliable. However, it can be a happy day as long as you can be by yourself now and then.

Tuesday the 7th. It may be time to do some work on any tax or insurance matters that have been pending. You can find that some recent expenditures have depleted your resources more than expected. However, taking a few risks on a financial matter need not spell disaster. You may find that certain recent investments are now paying nicely and have been worth the wait.

Wednesday the 8th. A journey should be planned with care. You may enjoy a discussion in which you participate or a lecture you attend. This can be a good day for new students. Meeting others with like interests can open your mind to new ideas, thoughts, and influences. You may feel a little annoyed by an in-law's overbearing attitude.

Thursday the 9th. Your day can be most enjoyable, especially if you are taking a vacation. You can find new surroundings and people interesting and exciting. It can be a good time to make a new start in some study matter or something concerning a child's education. It may be a good idea to seek out the advice of a teacher or other experienced person about what to do.

Weekly Summary

Your feelings toward a mate or spouse will be very cheerful and positive now. You can find that taking a loved one out to a show or buying some unexpected little gift can work real wonders. It still is true that little things mean a lot. Your calmness and steadiness can make others feel comfortable with you. But you may need to get off the beaten track now and then and surprise a partner by doing something different.

This may be your week for winning a prize, being awarded a bonus, or otherwise doing well financially. You will feel that joint finances are working out a lot better, but some sort of worry still seems to be hanging around. This could be due to the fact that you have had a few letdowns from those who owe you cash. Some of you may be acting in a very detached and even disinterested manner about money and practical matters just now.

Many of you will now be starting a new semester at school or college. Or you may just be getting involved in a course of personal study and reading. It can be a good time for resharpening those little gray cells.

37th Week/September 10–16

Friday the 10th. This is a quite important time for letters and other communications. You may be trying to learn a new language to help with your studies or career. You appear to be ambitious and goal-oriented. This can be a most enjoyable time for serious hobbies and interests. Recent efforts and hard work can make you feel that you have achieved something useful.

Saturday the 11th. If you take care, you can persuade a powerful individual to help you. You can put over your ideals and plans to an interested audience. The day will be good for charitable and humanitarian work. Your career should be developing well now, and you are justified in feeling that you are making progress. A good deal can be done behind the scenes if you can get in touch with the right people.

Sunday the 12th. This can turn out to be a very relaxed and pleasant time for you. If you are involved with the public, you are likely to be popular and feel loved. It will be a good time to get involved in fairs, parties, or other ways of raising money for spiritual purposes and charity organizations. Your dealings with a loved one can be pleasant and polite.

Monday the 13th. Try not to be too gullible about a friendship. You may be deceived by someone you thought reliable. This will not be a good time for groups that meet for spiritual or philosophical reasons. There can be a tendency to feel a bit disappointed or disillusioned. Maybe you are just expecting everything to be too perfect and will learn that that is not usually the case.

Tuesday the 14th. An unexpected invitation to a date or social function can mean getting formal clothes. On the whole, you Capricorn people seem to like getting yourselves dressed up in smart clothes and looking good. It may be difficult to find the cash to finance a recent speculative deal. This may cause you some embarrassment and annoyance, but you can learn a valuable lesson from it.

Wednesday the 15th. You are likely to meet a crowd of young foreign people. You may be teaching or lecturing them or simply showing them the town as a guide. This is a good time for students. A party or get-together with fellow students can be great fun and lively. Lots of little trips can keep you busily occupied. A particular reference book may be hard to find.

Thursday the 16th. This can be a day for putting in a lot of immense effort. It can be a time for making a will or dealing with various tax and insurance matters. Financial interests tend to fluctuate a good deal just now, but you seem to have your finger on the pulse. This generally will be a good time for investments as long as you keep an eye on the constant changes.

Weekly Summary

Professionally, you seem to be enjoying your work and relaxing into a new or different job. Co-workers are co-operative and helpful, and this makes for a pleasant atmosphere at work. You may be more altruistic these days and may even skip charges if a client is hard up. However, this kind of attitude actually pays off, as people will be glad to deal with someone so kind and generous.

Socially, life can be rather changeable and exciting this week. You seem to have a good many irons in the fire and a lot of group activities, friends to meet, and so on. It can be a particularly enjoyable time for dealing with young people, especially those from other countries. You may also be more involved socially with academic types of people or those in the legal profession.

Dealings of a highly private nature can occupy you these days. You may put a good deal of concentrated effort into planning for the future by making wills and various other provisions for retirement. This is wise of you, but try not to get too obsessed with the whole thing.

38th Week/September 17–23

Friday the 17th. You may find that a particular professional matter needs to be kept secret just for the present. It may be wiser not to broadcast any moves you mean to make, especially on the financial front. You may want to beautify your surroundings in the office, shop, or other place of business. However, a boss seems to be set against any innovations, so extra tact may be needed.

Saturday the 18th. You can really come out of your shell this weekend and impress everyone. You seem to be more confident and positive about yourself than usual. However, take care not to overstate a point you are making, or others may get annoyed. The domestic situation will be good for hobbies and personal interests. You are likely to find it a busy time if you are at work.

Sunday the 19th. If you proceed at a steady pace, a lot can be accomplished now. Your attitude is constructive and efficient. People can really rely on you and feel that you are a source of strength in their lives that they need. Creative matters are favored. You are likely to be more ambitious and goal-oriented at present. An older person can give good advice based on years of experience.

Monday the 20th. If you have an interview this morning, you are likely to make a good impression on a special individual. A teacher or lawyer is sure to give you good advice. The afternoon can be a time for concentrating on money matters. However, you seem to have an unusually detached and disinterested attitude toward such things. Some of you will be more concerned with the observance of Yom Kippur.

Tuesday the 21st. A whirlwind spending spree is likely to leave you short financially. However, you are in a very reckless and generous mood these days. You can recoup any losses from some private work you have going. This may be a good time for planning and getting your records in order. You can have a clearing out of files, old correspondence, and so on.

Wednesday the 22nd. You may feel a bit tired and dispirited now. But this can just be a reaction to your recent active life. If you can relax, do so. Otherwise you could find yourself getting a sore throat or backache. You are likely to feel very uninspired creatively, so it may be best to leave such activities until you feel more like it. Take a break, and look for some fun.

Thursday the 23rd. Neighbors seem to be in a gregarious mood. They may invite you to some local party or a meeting. You may be somewhat reluctant to go, preferring your privacy just now. Just working quietly at what you have to do can please you more than the limelight at present. This can be a day when you hear some unpleasant news, which can shake you up considerably.

Weekly Summary

This seems to be your week for showing others just what you are made of. You are likely to have a real air of authority about you that is most impressive. Naturally, if you are seeking promotion or recognition, this can stand you in good stead. Make the most of your strength of character and dignified approach toward others. You will find that people look on you as reliable and supportive.

Money matters tend to fluctuate a lot and even are a bit haphazard nowadays. This may be caused by outside circumstances or even to your recent more detached attitude. You Capricorn people are often considered as materialists. But at present, you seem to be taking a less pragmatic and hardheaded approach toward possessions and cash. In fact, many of you may be using your money-making talents to help those more needy.

A more positive and determined attitude toward life in general seems to be helping you to communicate better with others. You can find this an especially good time for local activities. Neighbors appear to be helpful and even in a generous mood.

39th Week/September 24–30

Friday the 24th. You are putting a lot of effort into creative interests or hobbies. But you may demand too much perfection from yourself. This can be a good time for taking care of elderly people in a nursing home or hospital. Be careful not to tire yourself out too much by running around. You may find that your mind is buzzing with plans for a new position or even a new job.

Saturday the 25th. At the moment, you seem to feel that home is very sweet. In fact, a boss's very unpleasant and uncooperative attitude can make you feel like throwing in the towel at work. Take care not to get involved in power struggles or ego battles. You will feel much more compassionate toward others and may get involved in charitable organizations.

Sunday the 26th. Your desire to make changes to your house or yard may mean spending a fair amount of cash. But it can fulfill a long-term dream. You may find it hard to communicate with young people whom you may meet in your professional life. It can be a good time for really working out just what you want from life. A loved one is inclined to be demanding. To keep the peace, you may comply.

Monday the 27th. Be prepared to take care of someone in need. Your values are a lot more self-sacrificing now. This compassionate and kindly attitude may mean that you are inclined to be generous to others, especially any children who may need help or comfort. You may feel very disappointed by a lover's careless or disinterested attitude, but there is little you can do.

Tuesday the 28th. If you want things to be stable all the time, you will be out of luck. Changes can come about if a lover makes a sudden break from the relationship. Or you may feel that you yourself are tired of going on in the same old way. A child might be quite rebellious and contradictory. Try to be patient and remember that you once may have been just as difficult.

Wednesday the 29th. This is not likely to be an easy day for love affairs. The morning can be uncomfortably intense and dramatic at times. You may do better to immerse yourself in everyday matters and daily work routines later on. This can be a wise move and can take your mind off your problems. In fact, you are sure to feel a whole lot better by the end of the day.

Thursday the 30th. This is a good time to consider seriously what you need and what you don't need. Clearing out closets, desks, files, and so on can make you feel better in more ways than one. You are likely to be very energetic in this way. But be wary of accidents or carelessness with sharp objects. You may be exhausted by the end of the day, but you will have a real sense of satisfaction.

Weekly Summary

Dealing with property and real estate can be your major theme for the week. You are sure to have some mixed feelings about family happenings on Saturday when a Full Moon makes for some troublesome moments. This may be due to the fact that work demands are keeping you away from home and all the things you want to do there. Or you may simply find that you are at odds with other family members over a money matter.

Try to enjoy yourself in your own way a little if you can. It can be time to stop worrying so much about others and being so conscientious. Try to do a few things that are creative or even sheer escapist. Favorite hobbies may be gardening or craft work. This sort of detailed work can really relax you and keep you from getting so wound up with the children or loved ones.

Daily activities can be very exacting at present. You appear to be in a mood for clearing everything out, mentally, physically, and emotionally. So why not start on the house and give it a good cleaning and clearing out? Then you can get to see just what you really value and want to keep.

40th Week/October 1–7

Friday October 1st. The early part of the day should be especially favorable for you professionally. You may receive news now of a new job, a pay raise, or a company car that may come your way. You will be feeling very lucky and confident just now. In fact, it appears that a powerful ally is working toward your best professional interests. You probably will want to celebrate this evening.

Saturday the 2nd. You may have to help a mate or spouse in practical ways. He or she will be grateful for your steadiness and calm approach, especially when dealing with a difficult child. An authority figure at work may seem to be a bit unapproachable. But you will have to overcome any fears you may feel if you want to rise up the ladder of success.

Sunday the 3rd. This can be one of those days when you may feel misunderstood by your partner. It will be wiser to wait a while before trying to work out some professional matter. The afternoon is likely to find you feeling somewhat anxious and restless. Maybe you are expecting too much from someone or something and need to be less demanding. The person involved may have problems of which you are not aware.

Monday the 4th. You can find that a joint financial matter is difficult to straighten out. A group of people involved in your negotiations may not be playing ball. Try not to be too depressed by what appears to be a rebellious and uncompromising attitude on the part of a child or a lover. You need to remain firm and follow the course that you feel is right. Others will come around to your way of thinking.

Tuesday the 5th. Things will certainly look a lot brighter now. You can find that a recent investment is now paying well. You may be trying to arrange some private deal with a bank or company. This is a good day for those having some therapy. You will now feel able to divulge secrets honestly and be glad of some good advice. It is not a day for superficial attitudes; this is all serious stuff.

Wednesday the 6th. Take some time to prepare for a fairly long journey. You may have a lot of loose ends to tie up at home or work and should see to these if you can. You may feel a bit regretful about a neglected or missed opportunity in a financial matter. A new boss may come in and make various sweeping changes which need getting used to. Do not be too quick to complain.

Thursday the 7th. Although you may have some reservations, you are likely to find that youngsters are doing well in their studies now. It can be a good time to visit an older member of the family, perhaps one of your in-laws. You may want to discuss some religious or philosophical matters with a church elder or someone you respect as sensible and wise.

Weekly Summary

It may be pretty hard going if you and a business partner fail to see eye-to-eye on how to proceed with plans. It may be difficult to get your point across. Maybe you need to think things through more carefully before trying to win over others to your side. This seems to be a time when you are. likely to feel ill at ease, maybe even nervous. Try to have more faith in yourself as well as in other people.

Joint finances, business partnerships, and other monetary matters can do well this week. But you still seem to be coming up against some sticky patches. It may be that a certain friend or a group of people is being difficult about a settlement or investment. You may need to push on determinedly in order to get things going the way you planned. By Tuesday, however, you ought to see a lot of progress made, although nothing is likely to be out in the open as yet.

Students can feel quite pleased with their work so far. You appear to be really enjoying expanding your mind and broadening your knowledge and ideas. Students of drama or music in particular can feel more creative than ever now.

41st Week/October 8–14

Friday the 8th. Your present job can be a good deal more to your taste than your previous one. You may be involved in music, healing, or psychology work. Now you are more likely to put your all into what you do with little thought for self. It can be a good time for those who need to buy up bulk stock for business. Your ability to choose what will sell is likely to be discriminating and on the mark.

Saturday the 9th. This can be a favorable time for making innovations and changes at work. It may be that you now have different values and a sense of how to apply these to your career and professional life. You should get on well with an authority figure at present. A cheerful and lively approach helps a good deal when dealing with members of the public. You may receive some media attention.

Sunday the 10th. This can be a busy weekend for you. A good deal of work may be done behind the scenes, as it were. You may be involved in some sort of private work this morning. The latter part of the day can be given up to more relaxing and escapist activities. You can find that a concert or theatrical performance you attend lifts up your spirits.

Monday the 11th. A meeting with a group of people can bring out the worst in you. Youngsters you are teaching, or who are in your care, may be quite difficult to control. You may feel really tired and ready to throw in the towel. Maybe some of your trouble is your exacting or high expectations. Try to keep a good sense of humor. Shopping may exhaust you but will produce bargains.

Tuesday the 12th. This is likely to be a humdrum and ordinary day. Even social activities can tend to follow a pattern and may seem a little boring or mundane. You could take advantage of a lull at work to catch up on neglected small jobs. If you can take a day off, this can be a good time just to relax and do as little as you can. This isn't easy for you hardworking Capricorn people.

Wednesday the 13th. You will tend to seek your own company, which may be due to a need for some personal space. Or you may be feeling under the weather and sorry for yourself. You can find it hard to get along with an in-law. Any hard words will bring up a great deal of buried feeling. Try to be as detached as you can if you want to avoid bitterness.

Thursday the 14th. It may now be time to make a change in a will or insurance policy. You can find yourself suddenly involved with someone who is not well and needs to be taken to or visited in the hospital. A friend may seem weird but quite good fun. You seem to keep changing your mind so much that it would be best to put off a decision for another time.

Weekly Summary

You are likely to be a lot more goal-oriented and ambitious now. Your career generally seems to be in a process of change, but this seems to be for the better. You are sure to be busy, and your work seems to involve a great deal of solitary or unrecognized activity. However, your mood is such that you feel ready to work silently for the sake of others and not so much for the rewards.

Socially this appears to be a mixed time for you. You can be especially involved with charitable or spiritual groups of people. These may in some way upset you or make you feel inadequate. However, the problem may simply be that you don't communicate properly with friends or group members. Don't expect others to be psychic. You will have to try to be more detached and less sensitive when with friends this week.

After this difficult time, you will be glad of a little break and some peace and quiet. This can give you time to be alone and reflect on what has been happening. If you have been feeling ill, put yourself on the list to be taken care of as well as others; don't be so driven if you can help it.

42nd Week/October 15–21

Friday the 15th. This ought to be a time for making progress on personal and private matters. The morning can tend to be busy, even a bit hectic. However, you are likely to be left alone to get on with it. Later in the day, you can relax happily and enjoy some creative interests or hobbies without interruption. Those with children will enjoy playing games with them.

Saturday the 16th. You probably will be in a relaxed, calm, and quiet mood. You may prefer to read serious, even sad, books or watch documentaries on TV. A social arrangement may have to be canceled. Just at present, you seem to prefer your own company. Young people can be somewhat annoying, but a pedantic attitude toward them will not help to improve things.

Sunday the 17th. You need to be wary of letting ego games mar your relationships with others. Criticism may not be meant personally, so don't get too upset. In fact, you can learn a lot from an authority figure or from some public personage you meet. If you feel a little down and unsure of yourself, remember that everyone gets a day like this. Try to snap out of it quickly.

Monday the 18th. You are not usually a gambling type, but this day may be an exception to the rule. However, you may expect too much from a recent financial deal. Don't be too extravagant when out with children, as they seem to be able to twist you around their little fingers at times. You are likely to make an important personal decision now after thinking about it for a long time.

Tuesday the 19th. Unexpected setbacks, bills, and other needs can mean a big hole in your bank balance. Children may seem to need a good many items that cannot be put off any longer and that they cannot do without. You may hear news of an acquaintance that is worrying. It may be a good idea to phone or write a letter as soon as you can. You can feel dispirited at the moment and cannot help but wonder why.

Wednesday the 20th. This is likely to be a happier and more positive time. The morning can be favorable for meetings or discussions about wages with a boss or a member of the staff. You can enjoy a short journey that you have to make in the area later in the day. It can be very pleasant to attend a team game with your children or indulge in other sports activities together.

Thursday the 21st. A neighbor may tend to invade your privacy. This can make you feel a bit annoyed and even quite snappy. However, try to control this if you want to avoid unpleasantness. You can be very efficient and organized where creative interests or hobbies are concerned and should achieve some good results. You may be able to market something you make.

Weekly Summary

Your personal interests can be important to you this week. Although you will feel quite your usual cool and calm self on Saturday, some upset with other people on Sunday will seem to erode your self-confidence a good deal. This can be over some important professional matter, or you may feel that you have failed to give your best in some way. You need to be careful not to allow clashes of temperament to upset the applecart.

You may tend to be extravagant or even a bit greedy when it comes to spending this week. Every now and then, you Capricorn people feel a need to spend a bit lavishly and wildly. It worries you a lot, but you just have to do it. This can be a time for a little wager on the horses or some other gamble. But don't expect too much from it except a bit of fun. Wednesday can be a luckier time for financial matters.

You may need to get out and about a good deal more at the end of the weekly period. It may just be small local journeys. Although you may have a few transport problems such as a car breaking down, you seem to have things organized and reasonably well under control.

43rd Week/October 22–28

Friday the 22nd. A chat with a neighbor can be helpful. You may get an invitation to a local gathering. A youngster can be helpful in finding something you have lost. Meetings and lectures that you attend this morning will be worth your time. The afternoon is good for those helping with charity work and collecting money to help others more needy. People are inclined to be generous these days.

Saturday the 23rd. You may get really annoyed with a member of your family. But the real reason for being irritable may be due to a recent clash with a boss or other authority figure. A parent may also be acting in a somewhat overbearing manner. You can feel very energetic and plan to do a good deal to the house or yard. But the family may have quite different ideas.

Sunday the 24th. Although it can seem to be time for some pleasure or light entertainment in your life, you may be bound for disappointment. A theatrical show may be nothing like you expect. However, a journey to a distant town for a concert or art show will be a good deal more successful. It can be a good time for dealings with in-laws. They will be more cooperative than usual.

Monday the 25th. You should be feeling a lot more energetic than you have in a long while. This may mean that you act somewhat erratically and try to cut corners. Take great care, especially when driving. You are more likely to be impulsive just now and do something foolish. You tend to be a bit harsh with a recent acquaintance about a debt or financial matter. Maybe it will do some good.

Tuesday the 26th. You may find it hard to express what you really feel to a lover. Early in the day, you can find that you need to reprimand a child. But you will be more inclined to take a sympathetic and less critical view by the afternoon. You can enjoy getting on with your usual daily activities. But don't waste too much time dreaming or fantasizing.

Wednesday the 27th. You need to keep your wits about you at work. Matters can get out of control when a machine breaks down. You may have to send an urgent call for a mechanic or electrician. This can be a good time for clearing things out. Some of you may decide to sell off certain possessions and make a few extra dollars. You will need extra cash in the next several weeks.

Thursday the 28th. This isn't an easy time for you Capricorn students, as you may feel bogged down with a lot of study and detailed work to do. However, if you just keep your head down, a lot of good work can be done. Praise you receive from a teacher can go a long way toward helping restore your morale. Your health is likely to be good although you may tend to overindulge in hot and spicy food.

Weekly Summary

Those of you who are interested in home and property matters can find yourselves involved in pressing problems this week. You may have some urgent and important repairs to see to. Trying to do it all yourself is not a good idea. You can wind up feeling irritable and exhausted. A clash with a parental figure or an older child may make you angry and careless. However, this can be a good time to make necessary changes to the home and surroundings.

If you can take a little time off from all your activities to have some fun, do so. You really do need to get going on some pleasurable activity or sport that can help you feel fit and cheerful. You seem at times to have a spell of bad luck or depression. But a pleasure trip, concert, or musical show can go a long way toward making you feel better.

Your everyday activities will soon claim your attention again. Colleagues at work may appear to be in some sort of difficulty and you may be needed to help to clear things up. You are likely to need to use all your tact and diplomacy when it comes to sorting out a matter of politics at work. Take care of your health this week, as you may feel decidely under the weather.

44th Week/October 29–November 4

Friday the 29th. Matters between you and a partner seem to be much improved. You can consider yourselves to be good friends above all. However, you may tend to act a little intensely or even jealously at times, which can be irritating to another. If someone upsets you, try to remain as calm as usual. Don't take things personally. It will all blow over.

Saturday the 30th. Loving relationships will really make you happy and restore your cheerfulness. The morning can be an especially pleasant time for being with loved ones. You will feel delighted with the progress of an extension to the home and redecoration. It can be good to have a lot of space. The afternoon may be kept very busy working out bills and making calls.

Sunday the 31st. Some recent confusion over a business deal or joint financial matter can need straightening out. This can annoy you, as you naturally would like a break. However, with a determined effort, you can put your mind to solving any problems. Try not to be too hard-hearted with children about their homework. They might need some time to play as well.

Monday November 1st. This can turn out to be a fairly uneventful day. You may spend some time working out accounts, seeing to bills, and sorting out papers. This can also be a good time to take a day off and just relax with your feet up. If you are at work, just keep going with the routine activities and enjoy the peace. Co-workers will not bother you.

Tuesday the 2nd. This could be a lucky time for you. If you are buying a new home, matters should go well. You can deal with a fair amount of money this morning. Some of you can look forward to a tax rebate, inheritance, or other sum of cash being paid to you now. The afternoon can be changeable and lively but certainly never boring, especially if you are a candidate for election.

Wednesday the 3rd. You will feel very energetic at the moment. Your ability to keep things under control and to organize others can be a virtue, especially if you have an older child's coming of age to arrange. This can also be a good time for planning any travel that can combine work and pleasure. You may be able to help an older person in some way. Perhaps you can pick up some groceries.

Thursday the 4th. A delightful trip can make the morning pass by pleasantly. Some of you may meet an attractive person while traveling. Art students may get a chance to see a master's works. Later on, you may need to spend some time alone working on papers, or accounting matters. You can achieve a great deal now both professionally and creatively.

Weekly Summary

You are sure to be very loving toward a partner this week, and it will seem as if he or she can do no wrong. But you may find that you need to guard against over-enthusiasm or being a little too demanding. Someone may accuse you of being selfish or self-centered when you insist on having your own way over something. But you can soon charm the person out of any irritation or temporary annoyance.

This is likely to be a good time in which to take a day off and spend some time looking over joint business matters. On the whole, you seem to be healthy financially and may now feel that it is time to expand in some way. This may include getting your shop or business premises redecorated and furniture moved around. The cost of it may be worthwhile in terms of improved business.

If you plan to travel now, make sure that everything is organized and under control. Some of you single Capricorn people may enjoy a romance while en route somewhere. If not, you can at least enjoy relaxing in style and watching beautiful scenery roll by.

45th Week/November 5–11

Friday the 5th. This can be a time for a determined attitude toward a professional matter. You may have to control your desire to push things along a bit too fast. Try to postpone making any decisions for a day or two. Your private ideas about a money matter may need to be kept to yourself. A contract for a book or film looks promising; you may even become famous.

Saturday the 6th. This can be a day when you feel a little unsure of your next move, especially in a professional situation. Should you push forward or hold back? Friends are likely to have a somewhat negative viewpoint; it may be best to ignore them and listen to family advice instead. You may take a pretty stern and cold approach toward a child; try not to be too hard on the youngster.

Sunday the 7th. Your attitude toward a particular friendship or group of people may seem muddled or unsure. You may find that you have been betrayed by someone you have trusted. Or it may simply be a sense that nothing is living up to your idealistic expectations. Usually, you Capricorn people are highly ambitious about yourself and life. But just now you seem disinterested.

Monday the 8th. Still a sense of personal failure seems to haunt you. Try to take a more positive approach and stir up your ambitions and desires. A friend or a child's bad luck can make you feel sad. This ought to be a time for making a new start of some kind. You may need to make a resolution to begin again with a group activity. But inquire whether others are still interested.

Tuesday the 9th. A private conversation with a younger person at work may help to restore harmony. You can feel a lot more positive about your ideas now. Musical and art interests can become a part of your professional life. You may sign some sort of contract or agreement. This can include a lot of traveling. This will be a good day for a meeting with a loved one.

Wednesday the 10th. Now you can feel as if things are lifting up again in your life. You may start to do a lot better financially with your professional contacts. Those of you who deal with the public can use your charm and diplomacy, which will be received. You may be able to fulfill some private or secret dream. This is likely to be a good time for lovers. Plan a romantic evening out.

Thursday the 11th. Family matters can go along happily and smoothly. There is sure to be a good deal of friendliness and warmth among you all. Your good humor will be restored again. A parent may be very generous in some way. Entertaining at home can be fun. If a recent extension to the home has now been finished, you will enjoy having more space.

Weekly Summary

You may be finding that your career is not going too well at the start of the week. But it may be because you have lately lost your usual desire to get ahead no matter what. Try to rouse up your usual sense of determination and ambition. Otherwise you will just get into a negative mind-set, and that is sure to make things go wrong. This is not a good time to make any kind of decision regarding your professional life.

A group situation seems to be in a state of constant change and fluctuation now. This can make you feel unsettled and a bit unnerved at times. It may be that little is living up to your expectations or dreams these days. But try to see just what really lies at the bottom of your sense of failure with both friendships and group activities. Make a new start and be as positive as you can.

The latter part of the week is likely to prove a good deal happier and to be more cheerful. Although you may be on your own a fair amount, you can have some space to work out just what is important. By Thursday, in fact, you will emerge from your chrysalis smiling and ready for everything.

46th Week/November 12–18

Friday the 12th. You will perhaps be too shy or cool toward someone you admire at work. It can be a busy time when dealings with the public can get to be too much for you. However, you seem to have a fair amount of personal energy available. This may be needed for a social function you are organizing later in the day. Most of the work is likely to fall on your shoulders.

Saturday the 13th. If you can keep up a disciplined and steady pace, a lot of personal desires can be achieved. You may find this a good time for helping children to sort out their career interests and give them a little firm direction. This also is a good time for making long-term decisions. A long-standing relationship or love affair can feel comfortable, just like an old sweater.

Sunday the 14th. A meeting with a young friend or a group of intellectuals can be quite intense. You may find that you have little to say, but what you do say is to the point. The afternoon may have to be spent preparing work or plans for the week ahead. It may be necessary to forgo some personal pleasure for the moment. Dealings with children will not be easy if you are tired and somewhat upset.

Monday the 15th. Your detached but firm attitude about a money matter can help turn the tables. You can find that a lover has a lot to say. Expect some deep and meaningful conversations. You are not likely to be in a chatty mood. However, there may be some group activities that you need to attend in the role of a leader. You tend to feel unsure of yourself or a little gloomy.

Tuesday the 16th. A recent decision or contract may need to be reconsidered. You may invite a group of people to come to your house. This can be a good day for making alterations or new additions to home and yard. You should be feeling a lot more effective and capable now and wonder why you were down in the dumps yesterday. It is a good time for teachers or lecturers.

Wednesday the 17th. Be sure to give yourself time when traveling anywhere. Delays and hold-ups can be very exasperating. Road repairs and other annoyances in your local area can make shopping or getting about harder than usual. You may, however, find that you are in a very determined and forceful mood, so you should be able to overcome any obstacles.

Thursday the 18th. A neighbor may be in the mood for a chat. But this is not likely to become a gossip session. In fact, you will have some important ideas to discuss with others just now. Your intensity and your air of confidence are sure to impress all who listen to what you have to say. This can be a good thing if you are involved in some local politics, which can get a little heated.

Weekly Summary

You have on the whole a steady approach to life and other people. This can stand you in good stead with any relationships now. A loved one is likely to look to you for help and support. You may also find that a determined and disciplined public face can land you a new job or otherwise help you to fulfill some personal ambition or desire. You seem to have regained your balance and feel more like yourself again.

Slowly but surely, you will now find that you are in a position to reverse some of your recent financial setbacks and losses. So make the most of a few lucky breaks this week, and get your bank balance in order again. You can do well with property or real estate. Don't be too cautious when it comes to signing an agreement on Tuesday. You may pass on your doubts to another and delay matters yet again.

Neighborhood interests and local politics seem to be firing you up with some passion this week. This can mean going to talk with others and raising some kind of protest about local conditions and so on. You appear to have some very convincing and deeply felt ideas to communicate.

47th Week/November 19–25

Friday the 19th. Things seem to be happy and cheerful at home. You may have some ideal home in mind and feel determined to achieve it. This can mean spending a bit of cash on improvements to an existing one, or you may consider making a move from your present abode. This is a good time for sitting down quietly and considering what sort of presents you intend to give for Christmas.

Saturday the 20th. A work situation may interfere with some family entertainment. This can cause you a little indecision or unease. You may feel that money needs are overcoming pleasure, unfortunately. Those of you who are involved in do-it-yourself activities about the home have to take care not to have a fall or injury. Be sure to take a break when needed. Do not just keep going.

Sunday the 21st. This is likely to be an expansive and happy time for family affairs. You will enjoy the morning when you may have some sort of religious ceremony in your home. The day is good for all spiritual activities. You may feel a little deflated or tired this afternoon. But this may be due to having to be out so much early in the day. A romance started at work seems to be going well.

Monday the 22nd. Take things slowly now to prevent overstraining yourself. Unexpected happenings may throw you and mess up your routine. You may be invited to various social happenings. However, you don't really seem to be in the mood to respond. Keep your counsel about a friend's somewhat dubious activities. Do not listen to gossip.

Tuesday the 23rd. The morning can be a far better time than of late for getting hobbies or creative interests finished. You may also have to deal with a child personally and positively. It can be a pretty difficult afternoon for getting along with colleagues. It may feel at times as if no one but you is pulling his or her weight. Lots of little jobs can need to be seen to quickly.

Wednesday the 24th. There is little doubt that all will go well with financial matters now. In fact, you seem to be on a winning streak. You may be in charge of accounts or wages in your daily working life. Or your interests may lie more in music and craft work. If you are selling clothing and art work, this should be a favorable time for such dealings.

Thursday the 25th. This Thanksgiving Day can be a special time for communications in groups and with friends. You may be quite absorbed in a book or a lecture you have recently attended. Generally this is a good time for any group involvements. Meetings are likely to be peaceful but not especially out of the ordinary. You can get ahead with routine tasks at home with little interruption.

Weekly Summary

Events on the home front tend to be harmonious on the whole. You may be working from a home base now, and this can call for a lot of self-discipline. However, this isn't likely to pose a problem to a Capricorn person. If anything, you may need some persuading from other family members to stop and have some breaks now and then. You can feel more contented in your usual environment these days.

You may feel more inclined than usual to throw yourself with some energy into creative pursuits after the weekend when family duties have been dealt with. This can be a good time for hobbies, but there will still be a tendency to push yourself to accomplish and finish things as if your life depended on it. You do need to be a little less driven and less demanding of perfection. The same thing applies to your attitude toward children whose homework may not meet with your strict approval.

The latter part of the week may be occupied with simple everyday tasks and routine matters. You will find that you are now benefiting from a lot of hard work and effort. Matters are sure to flow smoothly at work, and colleagues will make a better team.

48th Week/November 26–December 2

Friday the 26th. A reliable partner can help you out with a financial problem or debt. You may want to confide in someone about a person you fancy at work. You can find it hard to get on with work at home. But your sense of discipline and commitment is stronger than your desire to escape. You may have to practice a great deal of music or singing for an audition.

Saturday the 27th. A recent error in your calculations can get your accounts in a bit of a muddle. It may be a good idea to ask an accountant or expert to help out in private. You may have some tax matters or an insurance policy to straighten out. This can be a good time for those involved in therapy of some kind. You may respond well to a cleansing treatment now.

Sunday the 28th. You are likely to feel a bit dispirited at the moment. But don't probe too deeply to find a psychological reason. It may be nothing more than a shift in the weather. However, some of you may be experiencing sudden problems with a joint money matter or business deal. This can occupy your mind and worry you all day. Try to put it out of your thoughts until tomorrow.

Monday the 29th. This can turn out to be a far more cheerful and positive day. The morning may see your doubts and fears dispelled. Good news about a property matter can do wonders for your spirits, although there may be a lot of loose ends to tie up yet. Later in the day, you may have to see a teacher or spiritual leader in private in order to discuss a personal problem.

Tuesday the 30th. You may have to exert some willpower when dealing with your creative work. It can be important to try to get something accomplished and finished. It may be difficult to get some time alone to achieve your goals as you would like. Those of you who are researching for a book may find it hard to find all the information you need.

Wednesday December 1st. Ideals and aspirations can at last start to become realities. You can feel that you are achieving much more through your career now. Those of you whose work involves healing or photography and filming should do well. Your imagination is sure to be at its best. You may have to keep a certain deal under wraps for the moment, especially if it involves the media.

Thursday the 2nd. A busy but cheerful day can make you feel that you can achieve anything if you set your mind to it. You may be on a bit of a power trip just now. Take care not to overdo it, as you could upset a family member or a person at work if you do. However, on the whole, an exuberant attitude is good for you. Some of you may have to look after a child who has a health problem.

Weekly Summary

Those of you who want to understand yourselves better may now consider taking up therapy and psychology. This can be a good time in which to look more deeply into your own motives and compulsions. It can also be a good period for getting any joint finances in order. You are in the mood to reorganize things and to question what you see. Any money muddles and uncertainties need clearing up as soon as possible.

You need to watch out for various delays and problems while traveling this week. Matters beyond your control can set you back if you have a tight schedule. Some of you may be considering a late holiday abroad. But don't be surprised if something has to be changed at the last minute because of unforeseen circumstances. These may be of a political nature, so take heed of any advice or warnings.

Your ability to empathize with others can help when dealing with any tricky situations at work. You may have to comfort or counsel someone who has a prob-

224 / DAILY FORECAST—CAPRICORN

lem. It should be a good time for you, professionally speaking. You can incorporate any changes with ease.

49th Week/December 3–9

Friday the 3rd. You may feel it important to postpone a family get-together. Something at work can be claiming your attention in a big way. Expansion is the name of the game. You may need to discuss redecorating your home or office. You are really eager to improve your environment just now, but others may be less enthusiastic; you will have to talk fast to convince them.

Saturday the 4th. You may be a bit upset by friends' detachment and disinterest, but it will be wrong to take it personally. They may be worried by problems of their own. A function you attend tonight can turn out to be a real disappointment, but the spirit of Hanukkah will brighten the evening for many of you. Take care not to get mixed up with a weird group of people.

Sunday the 5th. At present, little seems to go right, however hard you try. This is not a good time for organizing or being involved in organizational functions and other social matters. You may simply not be in the mood for them. Or it may look as if everything is going wrong that can go wrong. A youngster's friends can prove very tiresome; you may want to break up a noisy party.

Monday the 6th. A deep discussion may need to take place between you and a young person. You can be quite intense about any communications just now. The afternoon is likely to be a little more free emotionally. You will be ready to take a more detached attitude by then. This is a good day for those who want to shop early for Christmas. You may find the stores less crowded now.

Tuesday the 7th. Your desire to be left alone can mean taking some time off or going on a retreat. You can find it a busy day if you are visiting folks in a hospital or nursing home. A private pension or retirement scheme may need revising and updating. The day will be good for those who want to start afresh in making a spiritual resolution or promise. Perhaps this time you will keep it.

Wednesday the 8th. Your exuberant friendliness and cheerfulness can be catching. Those of you who are involved in spiritual matters will feel bountiful and generous. You may tend to be a little unrealistic or over-idealistic about a situation or a person in a group. Try to get a sense of perspective on it all. Trying to get a home entertainment affair going can be quite difficult.

Thursday the 9th. This can prove to be a particularly happy and useful day. You are sure to be especially charming and delightful, though in a quiet and unde-monstrative way. You may receive a lot of compliments at a party or a musical gathering. You are likely to feel a deep sense of love for someone. For some of you Capricorn people it can be love at first sight tonight.

Weekly Summary

This is not a very good time for those of you who are bent on entertaining others. You may really wish you had never begun the whole thing. It may be that goods are not delivered, or people just don't live up to their promises of help. But all in all, you can fervently want to escape. This can be true of social functions you are invited to as well. Your detachment just now can make everything seem trivial.

Try to take some time off to be alone this week and enjoy some spiritual peace and quiet. If you enjoy doing yoga or like to meditate, make time for it now. Tensions will be sure to rise even more as the festive season approaches. It will be a good idea to get off to a peaceful start. You will feel a lot happier and more cheerful by Wednesday and ready to do good deeds, no matter what the cost.

This is sure to be your week as far as relationships and personal matters go. You are likely to have the right clothes and the right style and be just stunning now. A new hair style can do wonders too, and you are sure to hear the compliments fly on all sides.

50th Week/December 10–16

Friday the 10th. You can take things steadily and at your own pace. The morning will be a particularly favorable time for personal matters that may need finishing off and straightening out. Reserve some time later in the day for dealing with buying and organizing presents. You may have some surprises in store for an older child. It may not be easy to keep holiday secrets.

Saturday the 11th. Don't relax too much around the house this morning. You may have to switch into higher gear later in the day. It can be a busy afternoon with shopping, gossiping with neighbors, and other amusements. Later, you may enjoy a good film on TV or buy a video that you have always wanted. A member of the family may tend to be annoyingly unreliable.

Sunday the 12th. You may spend a good deal more than you intended, but it can be important to get a decent dress or suit for an engagement this evening. You may prefer to curl up with a good book rather than go to a party or on a dinner date. However, it may be professionally advisable to go, especially if some influential people are likely to be there. Keep your career always in mind.

Monday the 13th. This can be a far happier day. You can gain financially through a property deal. Or you may just enjoy reveling in the expanded space of a new home or extension. Family gatherings tend to be large and energetic these days, but they also are good fun.

You may laugh more today than you have in a long while, and that cannot be bad.

Tuesday the 14th. This may turn out to be a good time for dealing with some private correspondence. Sending a card to someone who is ill or in the hospital can be your good deed for the day. It can also be a good idea to get down to the task of writing out your Christmas cards and yearly correspondence. Be prepared for constant interruptions and annoyances. Computers may act up or friends pop in unexpectedly.

Wednesday the 15th. You can be quite intense and even a little jealous about a loved one. Try not to manipulate a situation to your advantage. You may find that a lover is not willing to play ball. In fact, someone may be acting in a very cold fashion and may make you feel rejected or unloved. On the other hand, it may be you who is playing hard to get. Chances of getting back together are only fair.

Thursday the 16th. An ego clash may mean that someone has to stand back and give up his or her position on a certain issue. And it looks as though it now will be you. However, you are not really in the mood to make waves and may prefer to take a background seat. Neighbors seem be having a lot of problems. Your sense of compassion is strong, and you may help them out.

Weekly Summary

Personal issues can raise their heads this week. You may find that your judgment on a particular matter is not as good as usual. You tend to be too optimistic about a certain family matter that affects you strongly. However, a sense of humor can go a long way. It may be necessary to avoid being too stern and unbending when dealing with others. You can strike people as a bit cool and distant at times.

Take a good look at your financial situation. It may

be important now to see just what you have available to spend and what you need to buy. However, there seems to be plenty in the kitty and your mood is a good deal more generous than usual. You need to buy presents or other goodies on Monday when you are feeling in a good mood and ready to please!

Although a lot appears to be going on at the end of this week, you seem reserved and tend to keep your thoughts and opinions to yourself. This is probably the best bet, as gossip or discussions don't get anyone anywhere. You may find it a trying time for dealings with relatives, but then Christmas always is. You are likely to be resigned and patient on the whole.

51st Week/December 17–23

Friday the 17th. It may be important to devote yourself to some spiritual work. You may enjoy a retreat or workshop of some kind that helps you to understand yourself. Home may be used as a meeting place for a group. You will be more involved now in humanitarian or healing matters. Your own health is likely to be good at present and your attitude positive, so it will be full speed ahead.

Saturday the 18th. You are sure to feel very happy at this time if you have a large family. All of them may be near you now, and you can feel very special. The afternoon can be a very enjoyable time. You may tend to fantasize a great deal about a lover. Your mind can revolve around secretive matters. Some of you will be interested in the study of the occult or psychology.

Sunday the 19th. Although you may keep a low profile, you can enjoy yourself in your own undemonstrative manner. A very formal function can be quite boring at times. Some of you would much prefer to be alone or with the children rather than out socializing. You may feel a longing to be creative, but little seems to inspire you at present. Holiday plans keep you too busy.

Monday the 20th. You will feel very compassionate toward a sick person or animal. You will enjoy your daily routine as a form of escape just now. It does at least get you away from family pressures. You may have evolved some strange or different values now and prefer your own company or that of a special friend. Any spiritual or healing work can bring rewards.

Tuesday the 21st. Don't knock yourself out having a clearing out at home or work. It would quite exhaust you and do your health no good at all. Some secret problem seems to be weighing upon your mind and it may be best to see a therapist or doctor about it. Machinery at work may have to be repaired, and this can hold you up a good deal. Working overtime may be a necessity.

Wednesday the 22nd. You will feel a lot more energetic and happy now. A positive attitude helps you to get over any recent health problem. The morning can be a busy but happy time at work. You will enjoy giving out gifts and cards to colleagues and receiving them too. Later on, you can feel oddly emotional, especially when with a mate or spouse. Put it down to the Christmas spirit.

Thursday the 23rd. The present is a good time for those of you at home. You can feel really secure and content. Children may have grown now and left the nest. Your pleasures in life, therefore, may be simple, and you are unlikely to want any sort of fuss this Christmas. In fact, in some way things can be almost ascetic. You can enjoy the company of a long-term partnership more than anything else.

Weekly Summary

Home matters are always important to you Capricorn people although you may seek to deny it. You are likely to see a few relatives this Christmastide, and this can be very pleasant. You may really be glad to be at home and give up all your many activities for a little while. Some of you may have family abroad, so that can mean that you have to go over to see them all or else have them over to see you.

Your enjoyments of life are sparse and simple these days. This may be due to lack of interest, a philosophical approach, or sheer frugality. However, you don't really seem to be a Scrooge. It is just that Christmas will mean more to you than mere revelry and feasting. Having the children away this Christmas may mean being alone with your mate, which can be pleasant in many ways. You can get to know one another again.

Take time to get going on all the little details that may be needed now. It can be time to sort out last-minute matters at work as well. Colleagues seem to be in a happy and carefree mood. You can exchange gifts, good wishes, and may even ask people to come to your place for a drink.

52nd Week/December 24–31

Friday the 24th. Early in the day, you and a mate or spouse can enjoy relaxing close to home and making plans. However, a party or other function this evening may not go as well as you were hoping. You may be angry with someone about a money matter. Be careful, as you probably are accident-prone just now. A lover may call you on an impulse and upset your peace and calm. But it will not really matter in the end.

Saturday the 25th. Merry Christmas! This doesn't seem likely to be as relaxed and happy a day as you hoped. You seem to be feeling somewhat despondent yourself.

A child or a lover may be the cause of your gloom. However, things can change rapidly if you put such thoughts aside and get into the spirit of things. Maybe you're just bored with it all these days. A call from a dear one can perk you up.

Sunday the 26th. A more positive turn of mind can help you to get over a recent disappointment. In fact, this ought to be a good day for enjoying family and loved ones around you. You may have a lot of parties or other social engagements to attend now. Make the most of them all and enjoy some intellectual conversations as well as fun and games. Children will be quite excitable.

Monday the 27th. Some of you may now be setting off on a trip that can give you great personal happiness. It may be the fulfillment of a long-term ambition. You can sound and look cheerful. You seem to have a lot of plans and ideas milling about in your head now. Some of these may be a desire to study or to take a course in something stimulating and exciting.

Tuesday the 28th. A call to a loved one can help to settle some problems. You are sure to be a lot more cheerful and happy. Being positive and giving of yourself can make a difference to your life. You will really enjoy a party, and it may be a time for romance and pleasure. Those with large families can feel happy to be surrounded by relatives. A belated celebration can be in the cards.

Wednesday the 29th. You may return to work now. If so, you will be in a relaxed mood. However, a boss may challenge you in some way. You should be able to show just how strong and loyal you can be. Try not to be too self-effacing. It is important to put your personal viewpoint forward too. This can be a good day for financial matters, so you can end the year on a happy note.

Thursday the 30th. Although a good many changes and new methods may be in the pipeline for your career, you can be a lot more adaptable now. In fact, you can see just how beneficial bringing in new equipment or other innovations is likely to be. You may have a raise in salary or earn some extra and unexpected bonus. You may hear that a superior has a high opinion of you.

Friday the 31st. This can be an unusually mixed-up day. The early part may be devoted to professional matters. You can put a lot of effort into getting things in order despite the pull of family matters as well. Later on in the day, you can enjoy a social evening with friends and see the year 2000 in style. In fact, you are likely to be in a most chatty mood and ready for some fun.

Weekly Summary

You may have to spend time working on firm or family accounts before you can really relax this week. It may be a time when matters need clearing up and getting into shape before the next year or before you take a journey. A lot of debts still seem to loom on the horizon, and you may feel a little cast down by this. It may seem as if you have worked so hard and had so little play yet still feel no better off in some ways.

However, such gloomy considerations soon appear to vanish. Although you may be on your own or feeling cut off a little over the Christmas period, others are sure to make you join in and be cheerful again. A journey to far-off places that you have longed to take may be on the agenda for some of you Capricorn people. This will mean a good deal of preparation and hard work. But now can be the time when it comes to pass; and off you go, full of adventurous spirit.

You can get back into the swing of working quickly if you are still at home. You are, in fact, probably glad to get going again. Sitting around is simply not your scene. Changes at work all seem to be for the best.

DAILY FORECASTS:
JULY–DECEMBER 1998

Wednesday July 1st. Excellent earning opportunities kick off the month for the Goat. Authority figures are likely to give you all the backup you need for a new or difficult job. Praise and acknowledgement come your way from upper echelons, possibly an immediate pay hike.

Thursday the 2nd. Business and professional activities should be straightforward and easygoing today. This is a good time to be doing some forward planning in career strategy. If a partner is spending too much money, don't suffer in silence. Speak up!

Friday the 3rd. A friend in need could ask you for some financial help today. It is probably best to give what you can and then consider the money a handout rather than a loan. If you suspect an associate of underhanded tactics, investigate the matter.

Saturday the 4th. It can be a frustrating Independence Day for some Goats if one of your plans is blocked. Do not lose heart if it appears that a dream simply will not come true no matter what you do. The intervention of a partner or close friend will help you.

Sunday the 5th. If your hopes were dashed yesterday, now they spring forth with renewed enthusiasm today. The horizon seems to stretch endlessly at the moment, and much is possible. A discussion with one key person should help you to put a new plan in place.

Monday the 6th. Be prepared to erect an emotional shield in public today. An onslaught of feelings will not be welcome, either to yourself or to the people you will be meeting. Capricorn is quite sensitive and vulnerable now. Seeing a therapist could be useful.

Tuesday the 7th. Do not waste time trying to catch up on neglected tasks when priorities need immediate attention. Emotionally, you are still feeling vulnerable. Almost anything said to you now could be taken the wrong way. Just assume that people are being straight.

Wednesday the 8th. Try to ignore minor opposition to your plans, for a partner may not agree with you or even approve. It is up to you to decide what will be the best course of action. The responsibility of having to look after a child will strengthen your resolve.

Thursday the 9th. Your partner may continue to oppose your plans. There could be some jealousy or resentment on his or her part, especially if you keep stealing the limelight. Alternatively, your plans might be seen as an attempt to distance yourself.

Friday the 10th. A feeling of being oppressed lifts today. Now you can set personal plans in action. People are likely to be helpful. If you are planning to buy someone a birthday present, financial constraints force you to be thrifty. Still, you should not skimp on quality.

Saturday the 11th. Financial pressures seem to mount now. Another budget crunch can interfere with your leisure activities. Some Capricorns will have to come up with an ingenious plan in order to pay off debts. Do not make promises you cannot keep.

Sunday the 12th. It is a good time for getting in touch with people you have not seen in a while. A favorite relative may sense your financial difficulties and offer to lend you money. Make a date with someone you find attractive. You will have to take the initiative.

Monday the 13th. You can afford to spend some time chatting and gossiping with people whose company you enjoy. Write or phone relatives who have been out of touch lately. Lay your cards on the table about an issue that is important to you. Welcome any opinions.

Tuesday the 14th. Guard against saying too much too soon in a new relationship, whether it is a personal or business liaison. It is possible that casual information will get into the wrong hands or be used against you by a competitor. For Capricorns looking for romantic excitement, good prospects may be around the corner.

Wednesday the 15th. Some of you have taken time off work to tackle repairs around the house. Try to work at a time that is convenient to your partner. Otherwise, there could be an atmosphere of discontent. A surprisingly good handyman's special could be found by the Goat searching for a new home.

Thursday the 16th. Avoid, if you can, discussing certain household problems or property concerns with your mate. This is a time when suggestions for change can make him or her feel insecure, and a quarrel might ensue. Some improvements will be desirable, but they can wait until everyone is ready for them.

Friday the 17th. Work and business run smoothly, and you may be daydreaming about tonight's date. You look forward to a romantic rendezvous. Increased intimacy results when you and your lover solve a few problems. Single Capricorn men and women are lucky now. A new affair of the heart will be invigorating.

Saturday the 18th. Gambling or speculation of any kind is best avoided today. You may think a big win is the answer to solving a money crunch. More likely, it will be a secure job that enables you to pay your bills and debts over a reasonable period of time. A love partner's luck could be better than yours now.

Sunday the 19th. Some Capricorns are not in the mood to tackle necessary work either around the house or in connection with your regular job. Worries and anxieties may affect your concentration. If you think long enough and hard enough, a solution may come. But if you are just spinning your wheels, switch off.

Monday the 20th. Money matters suddenly improve. Today's distractions can actually be helpful to your progress. A flurry of phone calls and correspondence alerts you to new opportunities in work and business. Do not waste valuable time reading junk mail. A meeting with a loved one will be intimate and reassuring.

Tuesday the 21st. Work will be more stimulating now because you have the opportunity to express your creativity. The nature of certain tasks will tap your talent in art, design, and graphics. A new affair of the heart is likely to release a wide range of emotions. The rapture and passion will sweep you away.

Wednesday the 22nd. If a romance has been rocky, today's developments will be reassuring. The relationship with your partner should be smooth and uncomplicated. If you are unattached, you may feel a deep longing for companionship. Why not call someone you have been involved with on a casual basis?

Thursday the 23rd. Today's New Moon is auspicious for turning over a new leaf in your overall management of personal money as well as money shared with a loved one. It may be possible to transfer a partner's savings into a joint account held by both of you. A loan also may be obtained. Try to pay off a debt.

Friday the 24th. Business should be moving along nicely, with the profit picture rosy. The end of this week is calm and uneventful, which affords you the opportunity to tie up any loose ends. Start managing shared resources with an eye to the future. The more money you and your partner can save, the better.

Saturday the 25th. Good news reaches you today. Some Capricorns will be honored for a personal or business accomplishment. If you are putting the final touches on a report or agreement, be diplomatic when it comes to expressing any financial questions or concerns. Choose your words thoughtfully.

Sunday the 26th. Changes of all kinds undertaken now are likely to yield a positive outcome. Traveling to a new resort or scenic wonder will be revitalizing. The best scenario for a trip includes a love partner. Single Capricorn people will be looking for eligible dates. Romantic opportunities open up out of town.

Monday the 27th. Right now the Goat is full of ambition and fired up with ideas for the future. Keep an eye on immediate priorities, which could otherwise start piling up. A long trip will be more enjoyable if you do not have to rush back to handle a situation that was left hanging. Keep busy if you are at home base.

Tuesday the 28th. A boss can be quite understanding now if you need time off for personal reasons. Secret plans you have been hatching can be brought out into the open. It is likely that you will receive the approval you have been hoping for. A plum assignment may be offered to Capricorn freelancers.

Wednesday the 29th. Rivals in the business world might make an unorthodox move today. You have a choice as to how to respond. You could adopt some cutthroat tactics. Or you could ask a regulatory agency to step in with a fair ruling. One thing is certain: you should not put up with any nonsense.

Thursday the 30th. Older individuals you trust are willing to give you good advice on business and finance. Discussions with other owners and partners in a venture will also prove fruitful. If you have been contemplating joining a group to start a new endeavor, today is auspicious to make your decision known.

Friday the 31st. Friends may have a habit of letting you pick up the tab for social or recreational activities. Make a point today of obtaining what your pals owe, even even though it may cause friction. You may wonder if your new dating partner's intentions are romantic. Ask! You will like what you hear.

Saturday August 1st. Romance glows when hopes and wishes are mutual. Today's news is good all around. There may be word of an impending wedding or engagement. Some Capricorns will make a secret romance public. Invite a companion out to celebrate.

Sunday the 2nd. Some Goats may feel extra sensitive and certainly high-strung today. It will be easy to blow things out of proportion. An in-depth discussion with someone you trust can help you solve a problem. Do not worry about money and don't ask to borrow.

Monday the 3rd. Make the most of a chance to rest and relax. You may have experienced more emotional strain this week than you realize. Burning the candle at both ends can only increase stress. A flash of inspiration shows how you can resolve a dilemma.

Tuesday the 4th. Behind-the-scenes business developments take a positive turn. Give long-range plans and ideas time to develop and mature. Avoid spending too much time reading nonessential or irrelevant literature. Later hours are significant for romance.

Wednesday the 5th. Do not despair if associates seem indifferent. Nurture your good ideas. Their time will come to reach fruition. Your guiding philosophy usually is one of patience. So keep thinking in a positive manner. Pay more attention to personal grooming.

Thursday the 6th. A change of attitude is likely as a result of speaking with relatives or neighbors. You will probably see more opportunities open up to you. There could be some confusion surrounding money owed to you. Curb spending for entertainment and recreation.

Friday the 7th. The ups and downs in your financial situation make it difficult to pay bills on time. There may be unexpected expenses in connection with child support or alimony. A talk with a former spouse will lead to some settlement of mutual obligations.

Saturday the 8th. On this unpredictable day you should not take everything a partner says on face value. There is likely to be some deception about shared finances. If you are trying to negotiate a settlement with an ex, the situation can become even more ambiguous. It is time to cut your losses.

Sunday the 9th. You will probably be happiest close to home today. What should be a short journey by bus or train could turn out to be more involved than you expect. If you must travel, allow more time. Your need to unburden worries and anxieties can be quite strong now. Be careful in whom you confide.

Monday the 10th. Significant developments may be taking place in the lives of your neighbors or relatives. There may well be cause for celebration. It is a key time for single Capricorn men and women. Now you can forge new links in the romantic arena.

Tuesday the 11th. Close contact with members of your family can be very important now. If you have worries and doubts, a parent or older relative is there to provide counsel and comfort. An unexpected financial windfall could make it possible for you to buy a car or make a down payment on a new home. Romance continues to be exciting.

Wednesday the 12th. Property negotiations that have been dragging on may be brought to a close now. Also, a business agreement can be signed and a new venture put in the works. A new stage of home life is beginning now, which can bring to the surface some long simmering resentments between you and your partner.

Thursday the 13th. Make definite arrangements if you want to fit in some entertainment or creative pastime today. Keep an eye on your budget and cash flow. Good news about money is likely to arrive now. Address any confusion in a business matter right away before teammates start off on the wrong foot.

Friday the 14th. Some Capricorns will have to juggle finances for the children's return to school. If you are negotiating alimony payments, diplomacy will be your best tactic. A passionate and romantic time is ahead for singles. A first date can be memorable.

Saturday the 15th. New or extra work that comes your way will take the pressure off mounting expenses. Your mate or a teenager may also earn enough money to contribute significantly to the family budget. A relative may come forward with a loan, or even a gift of funds. Do not ignore signs of stress.

Sunday the 16th. Good news about your partner's finances is a relief all around. As the money crunch eases, perhaps you can take advantage of a special offer to join a health club. Right now you should be doing everything you can to maintain good health. Use today to rest and relax.

Monday the 17th. A new partnership should be moving from strength to strength. Now you and your lover can put the attachment on a firm and permanent basis. Relative are very generous in this period. You may receive a gift of significant and lasting value from a loved one. A romantic success gives a sense of fulfillment.

Tuesday the 18th. Teamwork will be your key to success at work. Colleagues are especially helpful. You can even learn something useful from a competitor. It is a favorable time for preparing for an upcoming legal battle. Plan thoroughly and methodically. Minor difficulties in relationships can be easily smoothed over.

Wednesday the 19th. Affairs of the heart are highlighted today. Single Capricorns should take the initiative in romance. The one you like is sure to reciprocate your interest. An ongoing relationship may now enter a passionate phase. Mutual friends may already be planning an engagement party for you. Handle a sudden financial problem as soon as it arises.

Thursday the 20th. If you owe money, talk with your creditors to arrange a payment plan you can live with. Be cautious with spending until you are sure where you stand and know exactly what your commitments are going to be. In order to tie a complicated business situation, much clarification will be needed.

Friday the 21st. You are entering a new phase for financial security. It could be helpful to borrow money at a lower interest rate in order to pay off high credit card debts. If you have funds to invest, the acquisition of property can put you on firm ground.

Saturday the 22nd. New horizons start opening up now in terms of travel and study. It is an ideal time to consider continuing your education either for an academic degree or purely for pleasure. A long trip with your mate and children, or with a current lover, should go well. Do not let the past interfere with new romance.

Sunday the 23rd. You are at risk of becoming overloaded today. If there are too many social events to attend, it might be best to beg off from the least important or desirable one. A flurry of communications can upset the domestic calm. Try to get away from the madness for a change of scene.

Monday the 24th. A long journey can lead to an important personal discovery. It will be beneficial for the Goat to have time alone in open country. That way you can think, plan, and generally regain a perspective. A business agreement that has been in the offing should now go forward. Improved relations with creditors and other authority figures are indicated.

Tuesday the 25th. Business prospects as well as profits can be improved if you pool resources with other people. Make full use of publicity and advertising. A new marketing scheme can win new customers. Contact with influential people will be to your advantage. Clear up a debt in a timely fashion.

Wednesday the 26th. Steady progress at work is indicated. Meetings are useful for bringing outstanding matters to a fair conclusion. With the help of an ally or two, you can use a public forum to put new ideas in play. Later hours are favorable for a pleasure trip with a love partner or close friend.

Thursday the 27th. Friends are more likely to ask you for more money than to pay back an old debt. Be careful, as you could be setting a bad pattern by overlooking the money currently owed to you. If you encounter opposition from a boss or teammates, change tack until the business climate improves.

Friday the 28th. If a friend persists in ignoring a debt, raise the issue right away. But in business financial negotiations it will be important to avoid confrontation. Be diplomatic and tactful. If your partner is having problems with finances, he or she may turn to you for temporary help. Evening hours favor study pursuits.

Saturday the 29th. Loved ones and friends are willing to follow your lead for recreation today. If you are thinking about joining a sports or health club, a partner will want to sign up with you. Look around for special offers or added features that accompany the membership fee. Worries over money will be allayed.

Sunday the 30th. Rest and relaxation are just what the doctor ordered for leisure time. Anxieties about your health fade away on this promising day. The answer to a problem appears as if by magic. Past efforts to help someone in need will pay off in an unexpected way. Some Capricorns will receive a financial windfall.

Monday the 31st. Influences today are helpful for completing neglected tasks and reducing some of your debt. A long-pending negotiation seems to be near conclusion. But if you are hoping to close today, do not bank on it. There will be a few phone or fax queries to answer, as well as the final contract to be drafted.

Tuesday September 1st. The Capricorn Moon rising today is favorable for initiating new plans designed to stretch far into the future. Now your perspective is broad and your vision far-reaching. You can get your message across and attract followers. It will be fairly easy to convince people you are right.

Wednesday the 2nd. Key discussions take place today. Your persuasive manner rallies teammates around you. Now you can put a pet project into the pipeline. Catch up on the news from neighbors and relatives. If a close friend suggests a short trip, accept the invitation. A change of routine at the end of the day will be good.

Thursday the 3rd. Money, or lack of it, can be a great motivator. It's time to put in a request for a raise, especially if you think you are not being paid as much as you are worth. Make it clear you will take your chances in the job market unless your current employer rewards your efforts. Phase out overtime work in order to maintain good health mentally and physically.

Friday the 4th. Expenses may need to be juggled on this unpredictable day. Opposing influences impede financial negotiations. If you are thinking of applying for a loan, wait for a better time. A continuing problem has been fluctuations in your income. Adjusting your budget accordingly makes you feel restricted.

Saturday the 5th. Plan carefully how you will use your money on this long holiday weekend. Some Goats have saved enough to afford a brief vacation. Hiking and mountain climbing suit the outdoors adventurer. But take it easy, or you will be exhausted by day's end.

Sunday the 6th. This lively, sociable day taps the energy of the Full Moon at dawn. You may be up early preparing for a gala event at which you are expected to speak. Capricorn artists may be honored in some way. Those of you on vacation find renewed inspiration and creativity as you encounter the wonders of nature.

Monday the 7th. This Labor Day can be productive if you are shopping for something special, a gift perhaps. Spirited conversations with relatives and neighbors will put you back in touch with an important personal dream. You may have the urge to return to a place you once visited regularly a long time ago.

Tuesday the 8th. Nothing too surprising should happen today at work. Continue your efforts to turn a creative pastime into a money-maker. Concentrate on plans related to home and family life. If you are interested in buying property, look around to get a feel.

Wednesday the 9th. Family planning may revolve around the impending birth of a child. Renovating the house may be required to make room for the newborn. Expect some delay in property negotiations. An area of confusion needs to be cleared up. Avoid viewing today if you are intending to buy. You could be so taken with one place that you miss its basic flaws.

Thursday the 10th. You may have to act in a hurry to straighten out a financial complication. Perhaps you have forgotten that an important payment is coming due. Capricorn actors and athletes in training will be striving for perfection. If you are performing today, you may set a record. Short trips can be rewarding.

Friday the 11th. Your children will be an inspiration and pleasure today. One youngster may be honored for a special achievement in academic studies or athletic performance. A celebration is in order. Complications may arise at work and business. Messages can be fouled up, leading to all sorts of confusion.

Saturday the 12th. It is a useful weekend for making order out of chaos at home. First you and your mate may tackle the family budget, especially if you are increasing a youngster's allowance. Clean up and clear out unwanted possessions when you are neatening up. Designate items to donate to charity.

Sunday the 13th. You and your partner will enjoy an intimate and loving day together. All romantic relationships are deepened and strengthened. If there have been areas of disagreement, now the two of you reach a better understanding. For Capricorns wishing to start a family, this period can be a fruitful one.

Monday the 14th. Fortunate is the Goat who has the opportunity to get out of town for a while with a loved one. You will be able to combine business with pleasure on such a journey. Influences are very good for expanding your connections in overseas market. Those of you abroad, and single, are sure to find romance.

Tuesday the 15th. It is an enjoyable day for you and your partner away on vacation or even just on a brief sojourn. This fruitful time will be memorable for those of you intending to start a family and raise children. There are increased opportunities for single Capricorns to find true romance. Shared academic interests bring you closer to someone you have been admiring.

Wednesday the 16th. Keep plugging away to get a new venture off the ground. Dig deep in order to clarify a financial situation. If you are thinking of going into business with a partner, in-depth discussions will help solidify mutual goals and strategies. Carefully monitor your personal and professional expenses.

Thursday the 17th. Business as well as home life proceeds undisturbed. Look at your cash flow forecast and do some planning for the future with the whole family in mind. If you do not have a retirement scheme set up, think about investing in one now.

Friday the 18th. A change of scene is indicated, perhaps an early trip away from home base. Accommodations could become available. Single Goats at a resort will find romance exciting. Some Capricorns will be resuming plans to go back to school, possibly for an advanced academic degree or extra job training.

Saturday the 19th. Trips and scenic drives may be the highlight of the day, and will be refreshing. A wooded environment is very beneficial for Capricorns stuck in the city most of the time. Make arrangements to visit friends who have a summer place. Lovely surroundings will reach something deep inside you.

Sunday the 20th. Today's New Moon signals a new phase for Capricorn growth and development. Consciously strive to broaden your horizons. Take up a new interest, study a foreign language. Furthering your education will be beneficial. School and college will be intellectually stimulating as well as give you additional qualifications to improve your career prospects.

Monday the 21st. If you are trying to straighten out a financial mess, consult older individuals with years of experience managing money. It is a favorable day to put in for a raise in pay. You may already be in line for a promotion with a hike in salary.

Tuesday the 22nd. The Capricorn career is looking increasingly positive. There may be an opportunity to enter into a lucrative business partnership. It could move you into a new era of work and study. Financial consultants as well as lawyers may have some unusual advice that would speed a settlement out of court.

Wednesday the 23rd. Confusion and delay may impede an employment contract or teaching tenure. Be patient, as the agreement will soon be signed. If you are going on a job interview, ask the questions that are on your mind. Do not be thrown off course by individuals trying to blind you with irrelevant information.

Thursday the 24th. You can do much to maintain loyalty and trust in your friendships. This is a favorable time for calling people you have been too busy to see. Set up a few appointments to meet this week or over the weekend. If a long journey is on the agenda, use public transport. Health news is cheering.

Friday the 25th. Good company is the best medicine for low spirits. Organize an outing for loved ones as the weekend draws near. A close friend will be an inspiration if you are trying to get a new plan off the ground. The pace slows somewhat in later hours and will be ideal for reflection and study.

Saturday the 26th. Make the most of the weekend break to develop a pet project that one day can be a money-maker. Don't waste time on people who would take advantage of your generosity. Some individuals do deserve a helping hand, while others are plainly freeloaders. A library or museum archive will be helpful.

Sunday the 27th. Guarantee that you have peace and quiet today. It may be necessary to use the answering machine or unplug the phone altogether. If you invite relatives or neighbors over for refreshments or a meal, keep an eye on the time. Some individuals will overstay their welcome. It is up to you to draw the line.

Monday the 28th. Today's early Capricorn Moon sharpens your focus and increases your powers of concentration. You can zoom in on any plan and see how best to put it into execution. Romance is accented on this auspicious day. Your energy and enthusiasm intensify when you get together with a love partner.

Tuesday the 29th. Follow your own initiatives on this favorable day. You will be successful in communicating your ideas to influential people, which means you can get a pet plan rolling into production. Increased authority at work is sure to go hand in hand with a raise in pay. Capricorn money prospects are rosy.

Wednesday the 30th. Something magical is about to happen today. Renewed enthusiasm for a hobby or creative project prompts you to take it off the shelf and give it new life. An invitation to go abroad is too good to pass up. Cut back sharply on social spending so that you can save money for the journey.

Thursday October 1st. The shrewd Capricorn will be able to take advantage of fluctuations in the money markets, especially currency. If your personal finances are stable, seek to make some wise investments. An unexpected bonus or offer of new work is likely. The family elders are your best advisers.

Friday the 2nd. Be very careful what you spend shopping. Try to avoid impulse buying. Someone younger or a newcomer to the work scene can be an inspiration. Capricorns trying to formalize a new business partnership should make use of well-placed connections.

Saturday the 3rd. The weekend will be easygoing if you are in the company of loved ones. Greater involvement in community affairs will be rewarding. Relatives, friends, or neighbors who visit may be encouraged to join a sponsored event with you. If you have nobody you want to see, browse through the library.

Sunday the 4th. Church and school groups play an important role today. A teacher or a minister can be an inspiration. If you and a friend have books, clothes, appliances, and bric-a-brac to get rid of, consider holding a garage sale and donating the proceeds to charity. For Capricorn individuals who have been feeling alone this is a good day for networking.

Monday the 5th. A loan agreement may be signed, enabling you to consolidate some debts into one with a lower interest rate. But be wary of friends or relatives offering money. Their generosity will probably have strings attached. People are not likely to extend themselves without wanting something in return.

Tuesday the 6th. Seeing the world through rose-colored glasses is not characteristic of most Capricorns. But today's lunar influences could lead you down the garden path. Be on guard for deception, especially if you are intending to buy property. Ask a partner or friend to accompany you on any shopping expedition.

Wednesday the 7th. An irresistible impulse can plunge some Goats into a dangerous romantic liaison. Perhaps you are lured by the heat of the moment, a glamorous come-on, or merely a chance circumstance. Someone who flatters you may be up to no good. Whatever the case, bear in mind that you are playing with fire.

Thursday the 8th. Recreation and entertainment is featured on this easygoing day. You look forward to a theater event. A child in your life is an inspiration to the whole family. Today is auspicious for beginning a creative project or crafts hobby. Capricorns with artistic talent may be slated for exciting new work.

Friday the 9th. New work schemes devised by your employer may be initiated today. These could be accompanied by an unexpected raise in pay. Submit your plans for a reorganization of tasks and personnel. The boss may promote you to head up a team. It's the right time to join a health club.

Saturday the 10th. If you are concerned about a health matter, go to a recommended practitioner. If you have already seen one doctor, you might want a second opinion, particularly if you were not satisfied with the result. Love life is somewhat restrained now. You feel the romance has faded from the relationship.

Sunday the 11th. You and your love partner may have unrealistic expectations of each other, which can lead to resentments and recriminations. It is all too easy to accuse your mate of failing you. Skip the judgments. Look inside yourself and decide what you should be doing. If you have to visit in-laws, be pleasant.

Monday the 12th. Much of the day will be spent trying to put a love relationship back on track. Both you and your partner want to give it your all. There need not be a struggle for control. You both have good ideas, so compromise. Single Goats searching for romance should steer clear of individuals who are too pushy.

Tuesday the 13th. A friend might try to talk you into a get-rich-quick scheme. If you smell a rat, back off. Financial surprises today tend to be unpleasant. If you have a joint checking account with a partner, there may be a very low balance because he or she has been withdrawing funds without your knowledge.

Wednesday the 14th. An opportunity may arise to go into business with an older or more experienced person whose talents complement yours. It is also a favorable day for asking for help from the boss. If you need time off, it will probably be granted. Problems at home arise when a loved one is too stubborn to listen to reason.

Thursday the 15th. A renewed interest in health and fitness encourages you to free up your schedule in order to get more time for purely recreational activities. And today the urge to go on a trip is very strong. But the demands of your professional life warn against an early escape. Go out for exercise and mild sport later.

Friday the 16th. Today it may be possible to leave work early and get a head start on a weekend break. Some Goats will be fortunate enough to visit a wilderness site, which always appeals to you. Even with minimal funds you can enjoy the great outdoors closer to home. Focus on plans to advance your educational ambitions.

Saturday the 17th. A long journey will be a success in more ways than merely social and recreational. Some of you may be going on a weekend retreat, with the chance to experience a form of spiritual odyssey. For the Capricorn in search of metaphysical truth or deep personal awakening, an important discovery lies ahead.

Sunday the 18th. If you are struggling with an emotional dilemma, seek counsel from someone you consider honorable and wise. An elder relative who has seen it all will be a good adviser. New age philosophies may inspire you to choose an alternate career path or innovative way of making money.

Monday the 19th. Capricorns looking for a job should follow up interesting leads uncovered in the papers or over the net. Make use of your connections. An influential friend may pull a few strings for you. Workplace prospects for those of you currently employed are propitious sooner than you think.

Tuesday the 20th. Today's New Moon discloses excellent auspices for Capricorn's professional life. Important developments are taking place on the work scene. You could be given more responsibility with a corresponding raise in pay. An alternate job offer puts you in a bind. But a speedy decision is required.

Wednesday the 21st. A friend who has been working on your behalf is likely to get in touch today with good news. A frank conversation with someone close to you will help you resolve a career dilemma and make a final choice. Team efforts are the key to success in any activity now. The social scene offers variety.

Thursday the 22nd. Get loved ones involved in home improvements. Helping hands make any project more viable. You seem to be on the brink of an important personal awakening. Exchanging ideas will help to clarify your goals. This period emphasizes meaningful connections. Reach out in order to learn.

Friday the 23rd. Dim and distant memories can be coming to the surface today. It is a time when some kind of healing is likely to take place, whether physically or emotionally. Experiences you have been going through or are about to go through may link closely to the past. You may not be aware of the connection now, but in retrospect you will make sense of the process.

Saturday the 24th. There may be some confusion about meeting. Let people know where and when. A sports match can be so competitive you don't enjoy it. On the playing field of love, as well, rivalry can be a problem. A friend may horn in on your new romance.

Sunday the 25th. Take the initiative in romance. And certainly keep friends a safe distance away. A private and secluded spot will promote intimacy. Sensible advice to a youngster may keep him or her out of trouble, but may not ease the pain of adolescence.

Monday the 26th. You will be absorbed in long-term plans for a creative project. Focus on its potential money-making aspects. A new perspective on an old dilemma can be gained, especially if you get far enough away from the situation to view it objectively.

Tuesday the 27th. Visits from family members and relatives can unsettle your calm on this changeable day. Without intending to throw a money wrench into your plans, a loved one can offer all kinds of unwanted advice and suggestions. Accept constructive criticisms.

Wednesday the 28th. It is another unpredictable day, but the influences probably will center around your financial situation rather than home life or work. Capricorns who share funds with a loved one never seem to know how much money is being spent and how.

Thursday the 29th. You may have to refuse a friend money. Get-rich-quick schemes are best avoided. It is not a question of what is in it for you. It is an issue of what you have to lose. One good thing emerges. A beneficial new alliance will be forged.

Friday the 30th. The health of an ailing loved one improves. This period in general ushers in a hectic social time. If you are planning to give any parties over the next two months, send out the invitations now. You may hear from an old school chum.

Saturday the 31st. Health news is mixed. The prognosis is good under continued care and attention. You will have your hands full answering letters and calls. Strange goings-on this Halloween may spook a few. Know where your children are going and with whom.

Sunday November 1st. A local event you helped to sponsor may be a big success, adding to your prestige in the community. A charity function gives you the opportunity to get to know new neighbors. A problem that has created anxiety for your family is about to be resolved. Health worries ease, so focus on money.

Monday the 2nd. Do some personal and business accounting. If you own your own business, start the inventory process taking stock of supplies and machinery. It is a favorable day for scouting through secondhand stores and discount warehouses. You may find truly valuable antiques and works of art.

Tuesday the 3rd. A change in your attitude toward a family member may be in the making now. The uncovering of a few secrets has given you an altogether different picture. There may be delays in property negotiations today. Having more time to investigate is to your advantage. Despite the pressure to buy or sell on the spot, it would be wise to postpone a decision.

Wednesday the 4th. Today's Full Moon shines on romance and pleasure. Many Capricorns will feel lighthearted and fine after having experienced a difficult time at home. Single Goats may thrill to a romantic liaison with a neighbor. Travel, however near or brief the journey, will be stimulating. It is also a favorable time for writing love letters and starting a diary.

Thursday the 5th. Vicious rumors may be circulating around the workplace. Pay little attention, since there may be no basis of truth to the tales. Honest, diligent labor will take you farther than shaky speculative schemes. Rewards will come from regular work.

Friday the 6th. If you are undergoing job training, you will have to cover the material quickly. Cost cutting and other economizing measures put extra pressure on you and your teammates. Get together with them and lobby for better working conditions.

Saturday the 7th. Partnership affairs are highlighted now. Discussions with your opposite number should be smooth and agreeable. Put in place mutual plans for the future. Single Capricorn men and women may not meet the lover of your dreams today, but you are reaching out to new people. There is a fulfilling sense of togetherness with friends and teammates.

Sunday the 8th. New life can be injected into a flagging love affair. A marriage that has fallen into a rut can be revived with a little imagination. Find novel things together that will not upset the lifestyle you both depend on. A little bit of variety, though, is good for any relationship. Share a creative project.

Monday the 9th. Home life can be bumpy when one partner is acting like a judge or disciplinarian while the other is behaving irresponsibly. Or perhaps a dull routine is getting both of you down. It is not easy to break familiar patterns, but it can be done. In a new romance you and your lover must work to overcome the limits imposed by different backgrounds.

Tuesday the 10th. A business partner may be acting against your wishes. Such opposition could create more dissension on top of the existing financial problems. More give-and-take is necessary in all relationships. Take a united stand with your mate when a youngster is clearly rebelling against family authority.

Wednesday the 11th. Good vibes surround business and property negotiations today. You might be able to conclude a transaction that has long been in the making. Partners will be now contributing a fair share of money and hands-on help in a joint venture.

Thursday the 12th. Plan a trip so that you can take frequent breaks. Some encounters today will remind you of past experiences that were painful or embarrassing. Being able to express pent-up feelings relieves your suffering and is the start of the healing process.

Friday the 13th. The no-nonsense, feet-on-the-ground Capricorn will not be dismayed by the superstitions that surround this date. In fact, you may feel invulnerable to any possible mishap or loss. Do not push your luck if you are engaged in a sport or arduous travel. Those of you on vacation may be tempted to gamble.

Saturday the 14th. Good company livens your spirits but also can lead you into trouble. Some companions are only interested in having a good time and wasting money on frivolous pursuits. Be wary if you are shopping, and be careful driving or playing a game. A new wrinkle on an old problem arouses anxiety.

Sunday the 15th. Slow down and take an objective view of career developments. Make the most of your influential connections. Talk privately with someone in a position of power who can oil the wheels of progress for you. Absolute discretion is vital if you are told confidential or sensitive information.

Monday the 16th. What is apparent on the surface may not be the force driving today's events. Look beneath for answers. Someone may be trying to cover up a deception used to lure your initial interest in a deal. Powerful individuals behind the scenes will influence certain negotiations.

Tuesday the 17th. A persuasive representative of a charity or community group may approach you for a contribution. Pursuing the request further, you may discover that a dubious organization is behind the fund-raising campaign. A close friend with whom you feel entirely at ease can be your best adviser.

Wednesday the 18th. Today's New Moon launches you into an exciting phase for social life. It is an excellent period for making new friends and forging new alliances. You will be introduced to people with whom you have much in common. Membership in an elite club automatically raises your status in the community.

Thursday the 19th. Quiet influences make this the perfect day to rest and unwind. Any mental or emotional strain you have been going through will start to show now. Arrange to take the day off work if there is nothing pressing. Behind-the-scenes activities will be rewarding, with an unexpected bonus or gift coming.

Friday the 20th. Today someone may choose to divulge a secret told to them in confidence. Whether you are involved or not, do not spread any tales even if there is truth to them. A clandestine love affair made public could cause hurt and trouble all around. There is also the possibility of uncovering industrial espionage.

Saturday the 21st. Some Capricorns may be swept into a wide-ranging investigation of wrongdoing in public life or business. Your innocence notwithstanding, unfortunately people are tarred by their nearness to trouble. Guilt by association is clearly unfair, but there is a lesson to be learned from it.

Sunday the 22nd. Capricorn emotional resources are formidable, and you have the inner strength to defeat your foes and rise above scandal. Self-confidence mounts as you see that you are going along the right track. Family members rally around your cause. Your nearest and dearest are your best supporters now.

Monday the 23rd. Make a point of circulating on the social and business scene even if you have to take time off from work. Exchanging views with trusted associates will bring the reassurance you need to set out on a new path. Communications and education in general guide you in a new direction.

Tuesday the 24th. It is an unpredictable day when too much advance preparation could actually work against your interests. Take things as they come, and except a few surprises. Do not bank on financial transactions going through as promised. On the other hand, some unforeseen money might come your way.

Wednesday the 25th. Success in a financial negotiation is nearly yours now. Discretion is vital. Competitors and rivals are waiting in the wings to pounce. Do not make your creative ventures known to anyone who would try to sabotage them. Capricorn students should work on projects alone. Classmates may crib.

Thursday the 26th. Put aside career and financial pre-occupations in order to enjoy this Thanksgiving Day. Capricorn honors the family and tradition. You can make loved ones happy today. A surprise guest can be a mine of information on your profession.

Friday the 27th. Do not be in a hurry to settle unfinished business. Everything will happen in good time, and a satisfactory agreement can be reached. You can't be in two places at once today, so cancel the least important dates. Influences are excellent for Capricorn athletes, artists, and academics.

Saturday the 28th. Early hours are lively and potentially lucrative. Negotiations can be closed, and a nice settlement will be made. It is a favorable day for shopping in general, and buying a home or car in particular. Later there may be a hassle with an official or authority figure. Romance can become tense.

Sunday the 29th. Compromise comes easily today between lovers and married couples. Mutual efforts to make the home more attractive will make light of heavy work. The glow of romance can be rosy for those in a new affair. Capricorns meeting in private to discuss a merger or sale have a competitive edge.

Monday the 30th. Some of you are in a stay-at-home mood, eager to complete certain household tasks and redecorating. Be aware that haste makes waste, and slow your pace. Duty may call some of you out for the day or overnight. A delay in negotiations is nothing to worry about, so try to allay your anxiety. Expenses for children are mounting. Better set limits.

Tuesday December 1st. If you shop for holiday gifts and ornaments, decide beforehand how much money you can spend. If you give in to impulse buying, you will go over what you can afford. A trip with the children will be enjoyable. If you have grandchildren, welcome the opportunity to look after them.

Wednesday the 2nd. A lucrative work assignment is worth competing for. Your reputation and reliability speak for themselves, but there is no harm in tooting your own horn sometimes. Influential friends can put in a good word for you where it counts. If family funds are scarce, encourage a teen to take a part-time job.

Thursday the 3rd. Today's Full Moon discloses good fortune in business and professional life. Some Capricorns will be in the money. A bonus may be announced. If you have been doing overtime work, fatigue might now be taking its toll on your health.

Friday the 4th. Early hours of this changeable day are useful for labor-management relations. It is likely that the terms of a job agreement will be acceptable to both sides. Negotiations can wind down leading to a signed contract. Romance becomes difficult later. A partner may be trying to get the upper hand.

Saturday the 5th. Influences today become more favorable for love and romance. Put an end to partnership squabbles by being the first to bend. Accept a last-minute invitation to go to a party. The single Goat can meet interesting people, one of whom may soon become a new romantic interest.

Sunday the 6th. Be tolerant of a lover's differences from you, and the relationship will be smoother. Be careful trying out a new sport. Don't take chances with unfamiliar equipment or on unfamiliar terrain. Youngsters may be reckless today, too. Even though they may chafe against parental authority, they need more supervision now to prevent mishaps.

Monday the 7th. Someone out of your past is likely to make an appearance today. A business proposition could arouse your anxiety. But a challenge is just what you need. Be wary if you are asked to put up the lion's share of the money in advance. Some Capricorn parents will visit a youngster's school.

Tuesday the 8th. It is best to hold your cards close to your chest in any kind of negotiation today. The other players will be cagey and attempt to mislead you. Stand your ground if you are angling for a new employment contract. It is a favorable day for getting a business partnership up and running. Be sure the finances and division of labor are equally shared.

Wednesday the 9th. All the work you have done behind the scenes is about to pay off. Your uncovering the facts will save you and your company money and heartache. Later influences are favorable for taking a journey. Visiting a place that once meant a lot to you can trigger many memories, both happy and sad.

Thursday the 10th. If you are considering a long trip, compare the various forms of public transport in terms of time and money. Or find out if a companion might go along to share the driving with you. Social activities will be tricky if there is a lot of drink flowing. Remember, no one who drinks should be allowed to drive.

Friday the 11th. A change of scene will be beneficial, and can divert your anxieties. Seek recreational activities that are light and distracting. Avoid heavy conversations, especially about money. Capricorns who need a loan will have better luck borrowing from a relative than from a financial institution.

Saturday the 12th. Acknowledgment of your professional achievements may be accompanied by a formal event. A bonus can be given early, and it comes just in the nick of time. Shopping with the whole family can be frustrating. Go off on your own for a while.

Sunday the 13th. Domestic harmony really depends on give-and-take and the fair division of responsibility. A family member or roommate could get very irritable. If an official is blocking progress, talk to an older relative who has experience and connections.

Monday the 14th. Great joy is shared in a special friendship or reunion of the old gang. Today you may hear from someone you have not seen in a long time. Be wary if you are approached for a charitable contribution. Do not be drawn into a con game.

Tuesday the 15th. Visit neighbors, nearby relatives and friends, and business colleagues if you have the time to do so. Conversations can be enlightening and revealing. One of your prayers may be answered. Capricorn has much to be optimistic about now.

Wednesday the 16th. If your career prospects seem assured, your focus will shift to the personal today. Romance takes precedence. An intimate, possibly secret, meeting is indicated for new lovers. Some financial gains now may come from someone's beneficence.

Thursday the 17th. It is time to get off a treadmill or out of a rut of your own making and end a long-term problem once and for all. A close friend in need of compassionate support turns to you. Your friend's trouble may also give you insights into your own dilemma.

Friday the 18th. It can be a key time for some kind of decision making. You still may be uncertain about the right path to take. But prolonged postponement will do no good. A family member will come up with a good suggestion or at least offer reassurance.

Saturday the 19th. With the Moon rising in your sign of Capricorn today, you feel more confident about setting out on a new path. Focus on a study project or creative venture you have let slide. Those of you with handicraft skills might make gifts for loved ones.

Sunday the 20th. It is another favorable day for pursuing personal plans, preferably on your own. Solitude inspires creativity, so find a private place where you can express your talent or craft. Besides, family members may be difficult if they want you to cater to their needs rather than focus on your own.

Monday the 21st. The Capricorn birthday period this month starts on a bumpy note. People are unpredictable, so do not rely on them to follow instructions or to manage routine in an orderly way. Family want their demands met, but are not willing to meet yours. If you need a favor, look elsewhere.

Tuesday the 22nd. It is a day of pleasant surprises. Parents and children can look forward to a harmonious outing. Extra money will come your way through a discreet source. Look through the mail, and you are likely to find a check or gift package. It is a favorable time for applying for a loan from your financial institution.

Wednesday the 23rd. It is the long view that counts now. Do not throw caution to the wind just because things are going well. A solid base will bring rewards for a long time to come, though you may not see them immediately. Do not run around crazy shopping. Overexerting physically can make you ill.

Thursday the 24th. The Capricorn imagination is in high gear on this day leading up to Christmas Eve. You have plenty of time to express your creative impulses either in gift making or in decorating your home. Make sure business associates know you are not available.

Friday the 25th. Merry Christmas! Love life and family life are the double features on this special holiday. Friends and neighbors will want you to visit them, but get your priorities straight. The needs of your partner and children come first. Do not try to squeeze in too many engagements away from the home. Being obligated elsewhere could spoil a romantic evening.

Saturday the 26th. Although not many people you usually deal with may be doing business today, you could get a surprise call from a real estate agent or lawyer. Good news about a property transaction or other settlement perks your interest. The day's influences warn against haste and careless decision making.

Sunday the 27th. The company of close friends and family members will be relaxing. Talking about old times and taking a trip down memory lane will be all the excitement you want. A youngster may become restless and irritable when adult conversation seems so boring. There are occasions to let the kids off easy.

Monday the 28th. What a difference a day makes! A deal you thought was done and delivered is up in the air again. Obstacles no one considered may arise. You may have to juggle funds to meet new demands. Social events will prove light relief tonight. Enjoy a birthday party in your honor.

Tuesday the 29th. The children in your life look to you for instruction and variety now that school is out for the holiday period. This is a good day to take them on an educational excursion where they can have fun as well as learn. Go somewhere off the beaten track, and you may find items to add to a treasured collection.

Wednesday the 30th. A present you receive could make your working life easier. New communications equipment will be invaluable. Save up for something you have wanted a long time. What started as a mild flirtation is becoming a serious thing. An ongoing romance shows much promise for the future.

Thursday the 31st. You may get a bonus. There may be a promotion scheduled for early next year. An influential figure has put in a good word for you. Pay no attention to romantic intrigue and gossip. The people who like to stir up trouble have nothing to go on. Celebrate a new and promising love affair.

FREE Love Advice

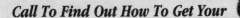

Does he really love me?

Will I ever get married?

Is he being faithful?

Call To Find Out How To Get Your

FREE Sample Psychic Reading!

1-800-686-5261

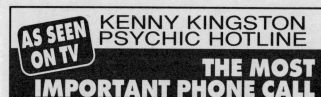